English 16–19
Entitlement at A-Level

English 16-19
Entitlement at A-level

Ros McCulloch
Margaret Mathieson
Val Powis

David Fulton Publishers
London

PR
35
.M35x
1993

David Fulton Publishers Ltd
2 Barbon Close, London WC1N 3JX

First published in Great Britain by
David Fulton Publishers 1993

Note: The right of the authors to be identified as the authors of this work has been asserted by them in accordance with the Copyright, Design and Patents Act 1988.

Copyright © Ros McCulloch, Margaret Mathieson and Val Powis

British Library Cataloguing in Publication Data

A catalogue record for this book is available from the British Library

ISBN 1-85346-214-4

All rights reserved. No part of this publication may be reproduced, stored in a retrieval system or transmitted, in any form, or by any means, electronic, mechanical, photocopying, recording or otherwise, without the prior permission of the publishers.

Typeset by Witwell Ltd, Southport
Printed in Great Britain by Bell and Bain Ltd., Glasgow

Contents

Acknowledgements
Introduction: English and Communications:
Entitlement at A-level   1

Part 1: A-level English Literature
1 Making the Transition from GCSE to A-level   7
2 Developing Autonomy: The Teaching Challenge   25
3 The Flexible Learning Classroom   53
4 Entitlement Areas: Moral Awareness   77
5 Economic Awareness, Political and Social Issues   92

Part 2: A-level Communication Studies
6 Developing a New Course: A Case-study   104
7 Developing Student Skills in a Variety of Media   111
8 The Communication Studies Project: Autonomy and
  Critical Awareness   123

Conclusion   134
Appendices   138

Acknowledgements

Thanks are due to colleagues who have permitted us to use some of the teaching materials quoted in the book: Mandy Dalton, Winstanley High School, Leicester; Kate Clarke, Northampton School for Girls; Dane Gould, Leicestershire Education Authority; Pam Hardy and Cheryl McLeod, Robert Smyth School, Market Harborough, Leicestershire; Martin Offord, Bilborough College, Nottinghamshire; and the staff of the English Department, Peter Symonds' College, Winchester.

We are especially grateful to Rob Powell of Network Educational Press for allowing us to reproduce material which appears in the *Enquiry Guide to A level English Literature*.

We have greatly appreciated help from Greg McCulloch, who made valuable comments on earlier drafts of several chapters, and to Deborah Thomas, who has given painstaking support with typing and layout.

INTRODUCTION

English and Communications: Entitlement at A-Level

In *English 7–14, Every Child's Entitlement* (Edwards *et al.*, 1991), an earlier book in this series, 'entitlement' meant making 'English in the National Curriculum accessible and relevant to all pupils'. The authors set themselves an ambitious and demanding goal, but their definition of entitlement as 'access' to a prescribed area of the curriculum was clear and uncontroversial.

Our book is concerned with post-16 education, a phase with a troubled and uncertain history in this country. There is no equivalent of a National Curriculum post-16 to which all students are owed entitlement. Instead of consensus and coherence (in theory at any rate) here is confusion and conflict, provision for young people sharply divided between the academic and the vocational. At this level, therefore, the term 'entitlement', as we shall show, has come to mean different things to different groups of interested parties, educationalists, industrialists and government ministers. This uncertainty requires us to examine the concept of entitlement 16–19 before going on to the definitions we shall be employing in this book.

Background

Industrialists have long been concerned about the United Kingdom's lack of economic competitiveness. This has been attributed in part to narrow specialization in both the academic and the vocational fields, and to the lack of integration between them; these features, they maintain, are responsible for our low staying-on rates and high levels of wastage. Teachers for their part have long been concerned about the high truancy rates and low motivation of many pupils in their schools. Both groups would concur that it has been the perceived irrelevance of the school curriculum to pupils' careers that has accounted to a significant degree for their disaffection. For the last 15 years much attention has focused on ways of remedying this situation as it affects the 16–19 cohort. Change has been most apparent in the field of vocational education, spurred to a large extent by the government's concern about a workforce which it felt was not ready to meet the challenge of the new technologies. The vocational area of the curriculum, historically low-status in contrast to the liberal/academic fields of study, has seen considerable innovation in the last decade. Some of this, as we shall show, has had beneficial effects on A-level provision.

The vocational curriculum

During the 1980s a range of curriculum initiatives were introduced which led to review and revision of the educational experiences of the non-academic 14–19 age group. To try to 'reclaim' this disaffected cohort of young people, pre-vocational programmes such as City & Guilds 365 and the CPVE were designed. Increasingly supported by funds from TVEI, an agency set up specifically to promote change at this level, these and other ambitious programmes contributed to a redrawing of the map of vocational education. The radical nature of the innovations can be appreciated from these typical features of the design of such courses:

- shorter units of learning with clear assessment criteria
- emphasis on skills and competences in the context of 'real work' situations
- a central role given to tutoring and guidance
- systematic formative recording of personal as well as educational achievement
- opportunities for active, experiential learning
- timetables negotiated on an individual basis.

The academic curriculum

Gradually, these changes in vocational programmes towards a more student-centred approach began to have some impact on the thinking of those concerned with A-level courses. By the late 1980s, government enthusiasm for 'enterprise' encouraged those eager to reform the academic as well as the vocational curriculum to hope that the time might be propitious for reform of the traditional A-level programme. There were two main reasons for dissatisfaction with A-level. First, because vocational courses have always been accorded low status in the British educational system, many parents, anxious about their children's future, endeavoured to place them on A-level courses. A large proportion of these students, though completing GCSE and A-level programmes, were not achieving particularly good results. Their chances of progressing to higher education were slim: often, indeed, they had had no such ambition. It seemed that they were doubly losing out; excluded from valuable vocational experiences that might help prepare them for the world of work, they were also denied the examination success that might have provided an alternative route to career opportunities. Second, senior figures in industry and education were expressing anxiety about the adequacy of A-level courses as preparation for careers at every level. The narrowness of the subject matter and the didactic teaching styles which had persisted despite fierce criticism by the Inspectorate seemed to them to provide an inadequate preparation for a labour market that increasingly demanded such qualities as personal initiative and flexibility, as well as a collaborative approach to decision-making and good communication skills. Initially responsive to this criticism, the government in 1988 set up the Higginson Committee which had among its aims the broadening of students' experience of A-level. Not surprisingly, there was widespread disappointment when its recommendations for greater breadth were rejected by the government.

Nevertheless, such was the groundswell of unease among industrialists and academics about the vocational/academic split and the narrowness of the A-level curriculum, that the search for alternative routes to reform continued. In was in this context that 'entitlement' began to be used as a defining word for the reform of 16–19 educational experience. Frustrated by government intransigence over A-levels, reformers redirected their efforts from attempting to change examination structure to the production of major policy statements about student needs. They were encouraged in these efforts by documents such as the FEU's *Towards a Framework for Curriculum Entitlement* (1989) with its explicitly student-centred focus.

Entitlement: first steps

Innovations in further education colleges had shown that it was possible to combine vocational and academic experience in the programme of every student, and there was growing enthusiasm for school/college links to provide a broader curriculum. These moves were accelerated by the demands of TVEI Extension funding, which obliged LEAs to produce statements of entitlement for all students in the 16–19 cohort. By 1989, issues of breadth, balance, coherence, continuity and progression figured explicitly in the curriculum statements of LEAs and their schools and colleges.

Given its student-centred focus, entitlement inevitably came to have a very wide meaning as LEAs considered, and asked their institutions to consider, the whole spectrum of a student's educational experience. This included the issue of access to programmes of study as well as the content of these programmes. For the student, 'access' was an aspect of equal opportunities: it meant having information about the range of post-16 courses available in all schools and colleges in her or his area and having the opportunity to make a free choice about which programme of study and which institution would be most appropriate. Once on the course, the student was further entitled to academic guidance through personal tutorials and to pastoral care. LEAs also required movement towards the integration of academic and vocational elements (including the introduction of core skills), exposure to innovative teaching and learning styles, and modifications to curriculum content that would give students an awareness of and an opportunity to become involved in issues in the wider world. (Extracts from LEA statements about entitlement are reproduced in Appendix 1.)

Implementation of these ambitious programmes depended on the enthusiasm of individual LEAs and their success in attracting funding for their schemes. 'Entitlement' was by no means a coherent government directive, though during this time various government agencies smiled on requests for resources to support those parts of the programmes that some LEAs, or energetic individuals within them, were introducing. Much of the attention focused upon the organizational aspects of the proposals, such as admissions schemes and tutoring and guidance arrangements, and most of the emphasis continued to be on the vocational curriculum. In a few cases, however, innovation did affect A-level courses. New schemes were encouraged by examination boards and took the form of modularization, as in the UCLES scheme and the Wessex model (Rainbow, 1990). In 1988 various Northern LEAs (Bradford, Humberside, Newcastle, North Tyneside, Sunderland) collaborated to investigate ways of embedding the entitlement curriculum in 14 A-level subjects. Leicestershire LEA, interested in and encouraged by this initiative, set up a similar project in 1990 to consider 11 A-level subjects.

These, then, were the ideas that constituted the notion of entitlement 16–19. Despite disappointment over the rejection of the Higginson proposals, there was some optimism in LEAs which had sought to broaden the educational experience of their A-level students. Their initiatives seemed to find further support during the period when John McGregor was Education Minister, and there was serious investigation of the integration of core skills into the academic curriculum. However, subsequent Education Ministers have quietly dropped McGregor's core skills proposals, even though the government's own Training Agency had expressed encouragement for the idea. The White Paper on *Education and Training for the 21st Century* (DES/DE 1991a) makes it very clear that core skills will not be part of the development of A-level. These traditional examinations are described in the Paper as 'successful and well respected examinations . . . steadily taken by an increasing proportion of pupils'. The government is committed to maintaining and controlling these examinations so that their perceived high standard is preserved. During the run-up to the general election of 1992, and since, much greater emphasis has been placed by government spokesmen on the excellence of the traditional A-level than on proposals to bridge the academic/vocational divide.

Entitlement 1993

The rapid changes which are presently consuming the energies of all those involved in post-16 education make it unlikely that there will be much time or space to discuss radical educational innovation of the sort described above. LEAs themselves may well disappear; the Inspectorate is in the process of being privatized; sixth form colleges and colleges of further education are preoccupied with incorporation. On the curriculum front, continuous assessment is being reduced, and in a climate where the 'gold standard' of the traditional A-level continues to be valued, any real widening of the base seems as far away as ever.

The problems facing teachers are formidable. The 'new' sixth forms have vastly increased numbers and many more students wish to proceed to some form of higher education. In such circumstances teachers could be forgiven for abandoning attempts to maintain continuity between pre- and post-GCSE teaching and learning and for returning to didactic teaching, model answers and dictated notes.

Such methods, however, are surely inadequate preparation for the world of work and for higher education. Industrialists are constantly asking schools and colleges to develop in their future employees a sense of personal responsibility and good communication and presentation skills. University tutors, of course, have always looked for independence, confidence and well-developed critical powers in the students they are recruiting, and in the very near future, these qualities will become even more necessary for students to survive and develop in the changing world of higher education.

During the last 10 years the proportion of 18-year-olds going on to higher education has grown from one in eight (1980–81) to one in five (1990–91.) The government is committed to increasing this proportion, with the 1991 White Paper setting the goal that one in three young people will enter higher education by the year 2000 (DES/DE 1991b). This increase in numbers in higher education is to be achieved without additional resources for universities. Numbers in lectures, seminars and classes have already increased significantly, and the intimate tutorial, with three or four students, is already disappearing. Unless there is some reversal of current government funding policy for higher education (and the government is adamant that no extra money will be forthcoming), by the year 2000 universities will be offering lectures to groups of 200–400 and seminars to groups of 50 or more. These are contingencies for which universities are already planning, and the modifications envisaged will require students to take more responsibility than heretofore for their own learning, both individually and through group collaboration. In such an environment, without the structure of the school's organization to support them, students who have not acquired skills of personal reliance and group cooperation are likely to fare very badly indeed. It need hardly be said that these are not skills likely to be acquired through dictated notes and the memorizing of model answers.

Since all the current indications are that the A-level will continue unchanged for the foreseeable future, we have to return to the proposition that it can be 'enhanced from within': that there *is* scope within the framework of the A-level syllabus as it stands for learning experiences that develop and extend students' self-reliance, sense of responsibility and ability to cope with the demands of work and higher education. The outlook for education today promises little reform and much continued disadvantage – crowded classes, narrow syllabuses, end-of-session cramming for examination, with little opportunity to explore wider issues in an informed and critical fashion. A-levels are in danger of becoming, for many students, inaccessible and irrelevant: at best narrowly prescriptive courses that will deliver them through to higher education, at worst a demoralizing struggle where initial lack of confidence may cause them to give up.

What, therefore, are the prospects for entitlement? It is our view that it is precisely *because* of the current post-16 situation that it is essential to give practical expression to the key elements of entitlement. It is important that students be given all possible opportunities to become active and responsible learners and to develop a critical perspective on wider society. Indeed, the government itself sees that this is part of the aim of the National Curriculum:

> . . . a broad and balanced curriculum designed to raise standards and prepare all our children for adult life . . . our children have only one chance

to receive the education to which they are entitled (David Pascall, Chairman, National Curriculum Council).

In view of this commitment, it would be sad indeed if after the age of 16 the nation's students were to be denied access to the entitlement curriculum during their A-level courses.

Entitlement: A-level English Literature and A-level Communication Studies

Our aims in this book are, therefore, two-fold: to show how strategies might be developed that enable A-level students to become confident and independent learners, and to show how, within the framework of A-level syllabuses, material can be introduced that will stimulate awareness of wider themes and issues. We have chosen to concentrate upon two versions of English: the traditional A-level English Literature and the more recently introduced, but rapidly growing, A-level Communication Studies. The individual preferences of many students have led them to choose alternatives to English Literature syllabuses. A-level courses in Media Studies, Theatre Studies, English Language and Communication Studies have all been attractive to students who have perhaps felt that the more traditional Literature syllabus did not reflect their interests. A-level Communication Studies combines the differing appeals of the 'new' syllabuses: involvement in texts other than written ones, project work, varieties of explanatory models (in this case models of how communication operates) and so on. Moreover, as will be seen, it is among the most genuinely 'entitling' syllabuses available to students. Its content investigates other subject areas of the curriculum and demands critical engagement with issues in the wider world, while its assessment requirements demand of the student a considerable degree of independent learning and research.

Part 1 of this book will consider strategies for developing students' autonomy and will introduce and discuss material which takes them beyond their texts into wider themes and issues. Part 2 will describe the introduction and development of an A-level Communication Studies syllabus in a sixth form college, and the teaching and learning programme devised by its staff. The Conclusion will assess the potential of A-level English Literature and A-level Communication Studies for delivering the entitlement curriculum to a broad range of students in the 'new' sixth form.

References

DES/DE (1991a) *Education and Training for the 21st Century*, London: HMSO.
DES/DE (1991b) *Higher Education: A New Framework*, London: HMSO.
Edwards, V., Goodwin, J. and Wellings, A. (1991) *English 7–14, Every Child's Entitlement*, London: David Fulton.
FEU (1989) *Towards a Framework for Curriculum Entitlement*, London: Further Education Unit.
Pascall, D. (1992) *The Guardian*, 6 October.
Rainbow, B. (1990) 'The Wessex Project: Post-16 modular developments', in Hodkinson, P. (ed.) *TVEI and the Post-16 Curriculum*, Exeter: Wheaton Education.

CHAPTER 1

Making the Transition from GCSE to A-level

It is central to the aims of the entitlement ideal that students be given confidence in their abilities as soon as possible in a course of study. This is, of course, harder than it sounds. Students embarking on A-levels tend to lack confidence in their ability to cope with the demands of the new work. Students of A-level English Literature tend to doubt their 'taste' and feel that the books and programmes they enjoy have no value in the world of 'serious' literature; they think that other students will know more than they do; they are daunted by the prospect of reading long and difficult texts. In short, they do not know what's expected of them, and lack confidence in the skills they bring to the new subject.

Can we carry out the entitlement aims and give our students confidence and a sense of autonomy at the beginning of the course? Can we start by encouraging them to recognize and value the skills they have and also develop these skills for the A-level syllabus? As importantly, can the new skills needed for successful A-level study be introduced in a genuinely 'entitling' way? In this chapter we shall set out a sequenced programme of activities and materials appropriate for these first weeks in the A-level classroom that will enable students to assess their skills and develop their confidence through discussion and collaboration, using their own reading and appropriate A-level materials. The activities which follow constitute the first part of the student handbook, which we see as a central entitling feature of the A-level course in the opportunity it gives students to construct and maintain for themselves sources of information necessary for their English studies.

The student handbook

Many English departments produce a handbook which is given to students at the beginning of their A-level course. It typically contains such basic information as: length of course, texts to be studied, assessment and examination requirements. The handbook can, of course, be more ambitious and inclusive, with a map of the course term-by-term, weekly timetable slots indicated, hints on and examples of A-level essays.

A handbook of this sort can be a considerable source of helpful information for the student. However, it is worth considering if it can be adapted and extended to become the first step of an entitling introduction to A-level English study. This can be achieved in the first instance simply by the way in which material is presented: rather than the closed format of an information pack, a more open, question-posing layout could be adopted which obliges students to find out information for themselves. Thus, rather than printing out syllabus aims and objectives, there can be exercises which ask students to find these out for themselves and go on to express them in their own words, as suggested below (p.10).

The potential scope of such a handbook might also be considered: it could be designed to accompany the student throughout the course. During the first weeks of the course it will be used for information-gathering tasks and induction exercises; during the main body of the course, subsequent sections will afford opportunities for self-assessment at appropriate points; while the final section could concentrate on revision skills. The emphasis throughout would be on two key entitlement ideas: information finding and handling, and self-assessment and targeting. Opportunities would be provided for individual and group work, with their concomitant skills, such as taking responsibility, working to a schedule, and collating and presenting information in a variety of settings. The handbook itself could be designed as a loose-leaf, sectioned folder. By the end of the course, students will thus have a record of their first steps, subsequent progress and final preparation for the examinations, a document whose outline will have been presented to them, but whose significant content will be their own, researched and put together by themselves.

The final section of this chapter will illustrate the range of possible materials for the handbook, and the ways in which these exemplify entitlement ideas. At this point it is appropriate to consider more fully the advantages for the classroom teacher of working in this way. For any teacher there is, of course, enormous satisfaction in seeing one's students begin to develop self-awareness; however, there are benefits of a more strictly pragmatic kind to be gained by following the programme suggested by the handbook.

At the beginning of the A-level course one of the most difficult, but most pressing, needs is that of assessing the difficulties likely to be experienced not just by the class as a whole, but by individual members of the class. If a student is not reassured about personal difficulties and encouraged during the first experiences of A-level then he or she may never regain the confidence to fulfil his or her potential. But for the teacher, time is short, and there is so much ground to cover in those first few weeks (and subsequently!) that it can be hard to obtain a clear picture of individual strengths and weaknesses. Often the first evidence teachers have is the first piece of written work. This shows to full advantage only those students who are competent writers, not those whose primary strength might lie in spoken argument and discussion of ideas. Moreover, the stresses of producing the first piece of written work can lead even the talented writer to strive for effects which disguise the natural flow of ideas. But it is precisely those naturally-expressed ideas that we want to know about, for these, rather than any half-digested version of what we might have said, are the truest guide to where our students are actually starting from, and therefore the best indication of where we should be starting with them.

We suggest that the handbook can readily yield just this kind of information to the teacher. Students involved from the first in a programme of discussion and self-interrogation are recording such information in the first section of their handbook: for the teacher, a glance through their findings will give indications of what students have found easy and what difficult and what they perceive as their strengths and weaknesses. Of course, they may sometimes be mistaken about this, underestimate their strengths, think something easy where they have in fact missed the point, and so on. But dealing with these kinds of problems is pedagogy itself, what we are all trained as teachers to do: knowing where they are in the individual student is where the real problem lies.

What we propose is that the students' handbook have a teacher's counterpart, in the form of a diagnostic chart that would help to 'place' students during the first weeks of the course, and suggest areas for development and appropriate pedagogic responses. The construction of such a checklist involves teasing out the differences between GCSE and A-level English, something notoriously difficult to do, since so often the difference is more a matter of degree and emphasis than of sharp distinction. However, if we want our students to think about what they bring from GCSE, and what A-level requires of them, these are matters we have to be clear about ourselves. Some of the differences that come readily to mind are the following:

At A-level:
- Larger number of texts
- Longer and more complex texts
- Texts from earlier periods with which they may be unfamiliar
- Need to study, discuss, write about 'in greater depth'
- Investigate significance of: settings, characters, themes, language, narrator; all of which raise different sets of questions
- Discuss, discriminate, evaluate, argue.

At GCSE:
- Limited number of texts
- Shorter time-scale
- Primary importance of knowledge, memory, ability to reproduce accurate information, write short and focused essays.

Thus at A-level, a typical question on the novel *Mansfield Park* would be:

> It is easy to admire Fanny for her goodness and to sympathize with her in her troubles, but it is not easy to love her. Discuss.

And on Antony and Cleopatra would be:

> To what extent can Antony be considered as a tragic hero?

And at GCSE, on Julius Caesar:

> Give an account of the market place scene in Julius Caesar and show what it reveals about the two orators.

On the basis of these observations it becomes possible to attempt a summary of the skills needed for successful A-level study. We suggest that the chart shown in Table 1.1, developed for and discussed by teachers attending INSET sessions on GCSE/A English transition at Leicester University, might be used by teachers whose students are working with the handbook to produce useful guidance for the learning needs of individual students. If the teacher works with a checklist like this while the students are following the first section of the handbook, then both they and she or he will have an appropriate view of strengths and weaknesses by the end of the induction period of the course. We shall set out appropriate materials for these first steps and invite the reader to bear in mind the dual focus of student entitlement on the one hand and pedagogic information and diagnosis on the other.

THE STUDENT HANDBOOK
Section 1: Syllabus and Induction

1. *Your A-level syllabus*

All A-level Boards print Aims and Objectives at the beginning of their syllabus. Though these are worded differently in different syllabuses there is usually much common ground. Fill in from your syllabus the relevant Aims.

You will see from your list that the Aims concentrate on such aspects as:

Knowledge and understanding
Personal response
Appreciation
Well-planned and coherent presentation

Discuss in small groups, and then with your teacher, what you understand by these processes, and make any notes that you find helpful at this stage.

Now look at the rest of your syllabus. Fill in what you can of the following checklist and keep it up to date as your course proceeds:

Number of papers in the syllabus
Number of texts to be studied
Texts chosen for study
In which paper each belongs
When they are to be studied
Length of each examination paper
Number of texts to write on
Coursework folder
Number and length of pieces for folder
Texts to be written on for folder
Dates for folder submissions
Dates of examinations.

The entitlement elements of this exercise reside in the opportunities given to students to seek out information for themselves, not just for one occasion but as a continuing task. Students are also, however, being asked to handle this information and make it their own by discussing the terminology of the syllabus and what it means for them. After this exercise, it will be appropriate for the teacher to discuss the students' ideas in a class session, both to help them clarify their own thinking and to foreground the induction activities which they are about to start. It will also enable them to begin to practise the skills they have been identifying as part of the A-level English study requirements.

From the start of the course, the A-level classroom should be a place where

Table 1.1 *Some reasons why students may find the GCSE to A-level transition difficult*

	PROBLEMS FOR STUDENTS	Y/N	CONFIDENCE	KNOWLEDGE	EXPERIENCE	PRACTICE	MATURITY	OTHER
			\multicolumn{6}{c}{REASON: LACK OF}						
(i)	knowing what is expected of them							
(ii)	understanding what literary analysis entails							
(iii)	having the vocabulary to express their ideas in speech and writing							
(iv)	doing literary analysis successfully in speech and writing							
(v)	synthesizing elements of analysis in speech and writing							
(vi)	having a knowledge base and range of reference upon which they can build							
(vii)	having a variety of reading strategies appropriate to A-level work							
(viii)	taking notes effectively from spoken and written material							
(ix)	managing their time effectively for (a) reading assignments and knowledge assimilation (b) essay planning and writing (c) project work							
(x)	effectively carrying out (a) research (b) essay writing (c) presentations							

students feel confident enough to express their thoughts and reactions to the texts they are studying. However, as we suggested at the beginning of this chapter, the intimidating nature of the texts, and the students' own doubts about themselves, may inhibit the free flow of discussion. How can this be avoided? The first few weeks of the course are crucial to the building-up of confidence, and if students are given the opportunity to be observant and thoughtful about their own reading and encouraged to communicate this in small group discussion they are more likely to feel comfortable about the transition to materials presented by the teacher.

The induction activities that we outline below aim to create from the beginning of the course a climate in which students can demonstrate and value the skills they bring with them from GCSE English. Students have likes and dislikes in their personal reading. They also have considerable knowledge about language and its effects, though they may not be fully aware of this. Sensitive use of carefully sequenced materials and activities will help them to understand what they already know and can do and build their confidence. Directed tasks of this kind, that encourage active class discussion from the beginning of the course and involve collaboration and sharing, help students to become effective learners who are aware of their own abilities and able to cope with the ideas of others. This self-awareness needs to be fostered, and the last part of the sequence asks students to review and define the skills they have brought with them from GCSE and assess these in the light of what they are coming to perceive as the demands of A-level study.

Induction Activity 1: Starting from where the students are

Ask students to bring in an extract from a book that they have enjoyed. (Emphasize that it is their enjoyment that is relevant here, and that no value judgements are being made about what is and is not appropriate to the A-level classroom.) Ask students to form groups of four or five and discuss their extracts, saying in each case why they have chosen them and what qualities they like in them. Each group should then make a list of 'Reasons for liking books'. In the next parts of the activity students are asked to reflect further on their criteria and are given a framework for valuing the extracts they have chosen.

Convene a class discussion to share the groups' findings and summarize with the class any common criteria. These can be printed on a wall-chart and displayed in the classroom, and students invited to add to the list as their course proceeds and they discover other reasons for liking books. They can also 'rate' their A-level texts against their class criteria as they work through them. Though this may seem a risky strategy, it is part of taking students' opinions seriously, which we must do if we are to be sincere about entitlement. However, this strategy can also give insights into features of texts (or even teaching methods we are using) that impede students' full understanding.

As a final step, ask students to assemble all the extracts that have been brought and arrange them in a sequence to be given as a performance during the next lesson. Students can decide on their own reasons for sequencing (theme, suspense, lively characterization, vivid prose, etc.), their own method of presentation, and whether or not they want to choose accompanying music.

The entitlement elements in this activity include making a choice, justifying it in discussion and collaborating with others to produce a group performance, all within a framework that emphasizes the opinions and views that students already have. The following activity uses a similar idea, in that it attempts to demonstrate to students that they already have a grasp of some of the ways that language works in literature, from their own knowledge and daily use of language itself.

Induction Activity 2: Response to a short prose extract

1. Ask students to work in pairs in the following way: with a partner, write down any sayings or phrases you can think of using the words: fog, mud, mire, lead. Write the meanings of the phrases beside them.
2. Re-convene the class, have some of the examples written on the board, and discuss the associations that the words have – do they refer to the weather, condition of soil, etc., or to more than that? (e.g., feelings, ideas . . .).
3. Give each student a copy of the first five paragraphs of *Bleak House*, explaining that the passage is set in London and that Chancery are the Law Courts. Explain any vocabulary they are likely to find difficult. Read the passage aloud to the students as they follow their text.
4. Ask students to read through the passage for themselves, circling each instance of the words fog, mud, mire, lead, leaden.
5. Now ask students, working again in pairs, to circle any words which they think associate well with these words (students will circle smoke, black, soot, undistinguishable, death, misty, etc.).
6. Working with contributions from the whole class, and using an OHP of the passage, circle first the key words, then, in a different colour, the associated words that the students have identified.
7. Discuss with the class the kind of pattern that is being built up (murky, muddy, lack of light).
8. Now ask the pairs to work together again, this time to discuss whether, when Dickens is using these images, he is simply referring to climatic conditions. Might he be making associations with other ideas?
9. If he is, what might he be saying about London, especially about the Law Courts and the Lord Chancellor?
10. After general discussion of this, ask students to read the last paragraph again: is their hypothesis borne out?
11. As a whole-class exercise, review with students what has been done, along the following lines:
    (i) working from a short list of words, common images associated with feelings and accessible to all of us in everyday language were put together by students, and considered by the class;
    (ii) these key words were found in a short passage of literature; further investigation showed that they were linked to a dense pattern of connected images;

(iii) the hypothesis was formed that, just as in familiar sayings, the images were associated with feelings, states of mind, ideas;
(iv) the final paragraph bore this out.

The elements of entitlement here involve information finding and handling, working together collaboratively on a task and then reviewing findings at the end of the activity. Just as this activity moved out from a basis of the students' own knowledge about language, so the following response to poetry attempts the same transition, this time by tapping students' knowledge of themselves and others, and emotional states.

Induction Activity 3: Beginning to make a response to a poem

Before students begin work on the poem, ask them to think on their own about the following questions:

Have you ever felt lonely?
What did this feel like?
Do you have to be alone to feel lonely?
Do you always feel lonely when you're alone?
Do you like being lonely?
Do you like being alone?
Do you ever hide loneliness?
In what kinds of ways do you do this?

In working on the poem that follows, form a group of at least four, and not more than six, people. You will need a cassette recorder and a tape. Here is the poem:

Not Waving But Drowning

Nobody heard him, the dead man,
But still he lay moaning:
I was much further out than you thought,
And not waving but drowning.

Poor chap, he always loved larking,
And now he's dead
It must have been too cold for him, his heart gave way
They said.

Oh no, no, no, it was too cold always,
Still the dead one lay moaning,
I was much too far out all my life
And not waving but drowning.

Stevie Smith

Read the poem in your group and after you have done this, assign roles to each person – someone to read 'him', someone to read 'the poet', etc. Practise reading together in role until you are confident enough to make a recording of your reading.

When you have done this, work on the questions below, either on your own or in pairs.

Stanza 1: Who is the speaker in lines 3–4?
What is unusual about this?

Stanza 2: Who are the speakers in lines 5, 6, 7?
Taking lines 4, 5, 6 together, what seems to have happened?
What effect does the short line 6 have?
Why do you think line 7 is a long line?
How many different ways can you say line 8? try to work out the implication of each different emphasis

Stanza 3: What words in lines 9 and 11 might cause you to modify your answer to the second question on Stanza 2?
Does the word 'cold' suggest only physical temperature? If no, what else?
What does the expression 'too far out' suggest?
From your previous answers what do you understand by the last line, and hence by the poem?

When you have completed the questions, meet again in your reading group and discuss your answers. Listen again to your taped reading in the light of your discussion. If you feel you could now give a more effective reading then do so, but keep the original one also.

When you have completed your taped reading(s), record on to the tape what effects you are trying to bring out for the listener; in other words, how you have spoken the words so as to convey what you understand as the meaning to the listener.

There are several important entitlement elements embedded in this activity. We have asked students to feed private reflection into small group collaboration: however, by asking them to go on to a further review in the light of questions on the poem, we are introducing the idea that revision and reconsideration are not signs of imperfect understanding, but rather of more intense thought, which always takes time. Finally, by asking students to prepare public performances we have enabled them to move through a sequenced activity (private – small group – public performance), at each stage of which they have been in control of what is going on, making decisions themselves about the ways they think the poem is working.

Induction Activity 4: Beginning research

It is encouraging for students to feel, at the beginning of the course, that they already have valuable skills. This can be achieved by arranging for them to make a contribution to the literature work of a younger age group. The following exercise was completed by students at Northampton School for Girls during the four-week Induction Programme at the beginning of their A-level course. We set out the instructions exactly as they were given to the students, and display their results.

Task: The National Curriculum requires pre-twentieth century reading. A Year 10 English teacher wishes to teach *Tess of the D'Urbervilles* to her/his group. The teacher has not got very much lesson time to devote to this and needs a quick way of (1) giving background information on Hardy's life and times and (2) a way into the novel, which is long, complicated and a little difficult.

Resources:

- video of *Tess*
- copies of *Tess of the d'Urbervilles*
- background materials
- school and town libraries
- photocopier (budget 50p)
- chronology.

What you have to do:
Produce study materials that a teacher can use with a Year 10 group and justify to the teacher the approach you have taken. For example:

- visual displays
- broadsheets
- simplified extracts
- extracts with notes
- lists of characters with illustrations
- dramatised reading.

Assessment objectives:

Selection of information
Awareness of audience
Appropriateness of material
Presentation
Planning and time management
Convey context in which Hardy worked.

Time to complete task: One week

The students worked unsupervised in groups, and staff provided the initial resources. The students had six 50-minute lessons and any other time they chose in the week to complete their task. At the end of this time they had devised a series of 'ways in' to *Tess of the D'Urbervilles* which, in addition to the materials shown below, included: maps and time lines, activities linked to a video clip, and a video made by the students of 'Hardy' talking about his life and work, filmed in a local graveyard, complete with dog and costumes. As well as giving this material to the Year 10 teacher to use with her students, the A-level students themselves ran two one-hour seminars for Year 11 students doing *Tess of the D'Urbervilles* for wider reading as part of their GCSE folder.

The results achieved by the girls indicate how entitlement aims have been met during this activity. Here we have confident learners working together successfully to a very tight schedule and producing work that exactly meets the given requirements set out.

TESS OF THE D'URBERVILLES BY THOMAS HARDY

PAGE 236 . . . THE CONSEQUENCE . . .

"Angel felt that he would like to spend the day with her before the wedding, somewhere away from the dairy, as a last jaunt in her company while they were mere lover and mistress; a romantic day, in circumstances that would never be repeated; with that other and greater day beaming close ahead of them."

PAGE 259 . . . THE WOMAN PAYS . . .

"He turned away, and bent over a chair. Tess followed him to the middle of the room where he was, and stood there staring at him with eyes that did not weep. Presently she slid down upon her knees beside his foot, and from this position she crouched in a heap.

"In the name of our love, forgive me?" she whispered with a dry mouth.

"I have forgiven you for the same."

And, as he did not answer, she said again –

"Forgive me as you are forgiven! I forgive you, Angel."

"You – yes you do."

"But you do not forgive me?"

"O Tess, forgiveness does not apply to this case! . . ."

PAGE 262 . . . THE WOMAN PAYS . . .

"Tess," he said as gently as he could speak, "I cannot stay – in this room – just now. I will walk out a little way."

He quietly left the room, and the two glasses of wine that he had poured out for their supper – one for her, one for him – remained on the table untasted. This was what their agape had come to. At tea, two or three hours earlier, they had, in the freakishness of affection, drunk from one cup.

The closing door behind him, gently as if it had been pulled to, roused Tess from her stupor. He was gone.

THOMAS HARDY
1840 - 1928

EMMA

Thomas Hardy met Emma Gifford in 1870 whilst living in Cornwall. Four years after this they were married. We are able to see that the marriage was very happy, for a while, from reading Hardy's earlier poems, where his marriage to Emma was one of his most popular themes. However as time progressed the marriage seemed to dissolve and they drifted apart. Again we know this from many of his poems. This is also reflected in the relationship formed between Angel Clare and Tess in "Tess of the D'Urbervilles". Emma Hardy died on November 27 1912. Shortly after this Hardy married Florence Dugdale and died on January 11

THOMAS

CONSCIENCE ALLEY

Now you have seen the video clip and have discussed the themes, characters and the influences in Hardy's writing imagine you are Tess or Angel Clare and begin to think about how they felt in this situation.

Half of the group imagine you are Tess and the other half Angel Clare and express your feelings through a conscience alley.

"I repeat, the woman I have been loving is not you."

"But who?"

"Another woman in your shape."

POINTS OF DISCUSSION......

1. Do you feel sympathetic toward the characters?

2. Do you feel Angel Clare reacted in the right way?

3. Would you react in the same way?

4. Do you think Tess was right to tell him?

5. If you were writing this part of the story would you keep it the same as Hardy or would you change it?

6. Do you like the way in which Hardy has written this part of the story?

7. Do you feel Hardy was influenced by his own marriage when writing this part of the story?

Themes

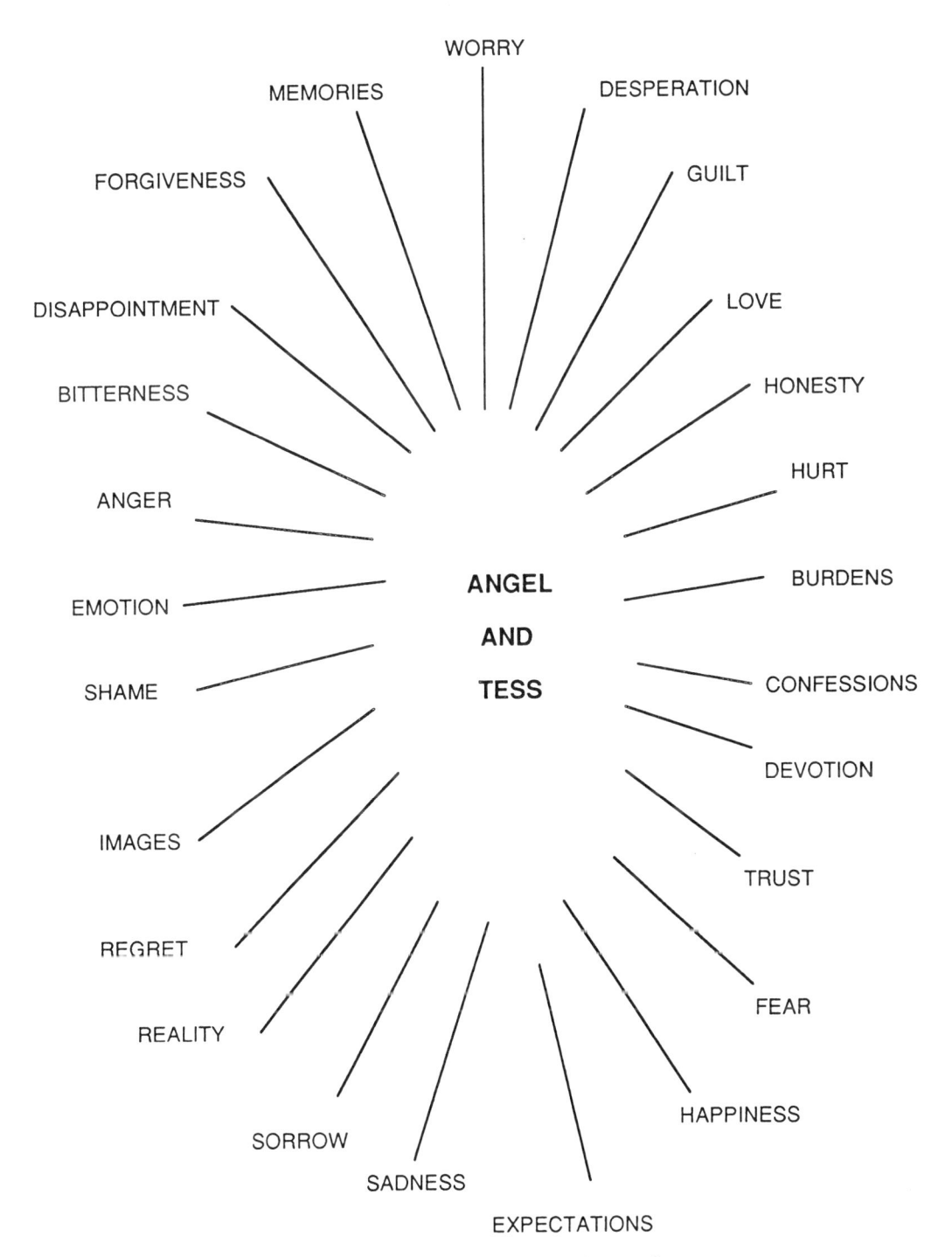

Spider diagram centered on **ANGEL AND TESS** with the following themes radiating outward:

- WORRY
- MEMORIES
- FORGIVENESS
- DISAPPOINTMENT
- BITTERNESS
- ANGER
- EMOTION
- SHAME
- IMAGES
- REGRET
- REALITY
- SORROW
- SADNESS
- EXPECTATIONS
- HAPPINESS
- FEAR
- TRUST
- DEVOTION
- CONFESSIONS
- BURDENS
- HURT
- HONESTY
- LOVE
- GUILT
- DESPERATION

Can you think of any other themes?

HARDY'S TIMES

Queen Victoria was on the throne from 1837-1901.

The 19th century was a time of great change both at home and abroad.

There were new inventions and discoveries of things that we now take for granted such as: the bicycle, matches, the postage stamp, the telephone, sewing machine and the photograph.

There was exploration of Africa, David Livingstone discovered Victoria Falls in 1855 and there was also exploration of Australia. The 'arts' gave us such composers as Chopin and Tchaikovsky, writers like Robert Louis Stevenson and the Brontë sisters, among others. It was also the age of painters like Van Gogh.

There were several important world events such as the abolition of slavery in Great Britain and the United States of America, the Crimean War, the American Civil War and the opening of the Suez Canal.

DID THESE EVENTS HAVE MUCH EFFECT ON RURAL LIFE IN ENGLAND?

The Industrial Revolution in England had a great effect on farming – there were now machines that could do a job quicker and more reliably than previously. However, this hadn't made too much difference to the lifestyle of farmers and labourers.

In the country, poor labourers with large families sometimes lived in small cottages made of mud, plaster and thatch. They had one room up and one down. Even families with 10 or 12 children crowded into that space.

At the earliest possible age, the children in the family would be sent out to work to help support the family.

There was very little time for relaxation as working hours were long, and then for a wife there was probably a large family to care for.

The lifestyle was very different from today. Sanitation was bad, many houses only had an earth closet and cesspool. Also, people seldom took a bath. Homes were lit by candles and oil lamps although as the century progressed gas lighting was introduced to certain towns.

The poor had a very different diet compared to the middle classes, they lived mainly on meat, bread, potatoes and a few vegetables. In rural areas poaching was common practice as they tried to save their families from starvation.

Induction Activity 5: Personal review

Students can benefit even at this early stage in the course from a self-assessment exercise that draws on activities like the foregoing, completed during the induction period. The following questionnaire enables students to measure their achievements during these introductory lessons:

Student Self-review Sheet

It is important for you to reflect upon the qualities and skills you have identified in yourself and have been using during the sequence of activities that you've been engaged on. This will help you set targets for your future study and will also give you confidence in yourself as an A-level student. Discuss your feelings about yourself with other students in your group, and try to come to a realistic view of your progress. The following list may help you to focus your thoughts, but add any other ideas that you have about yourself or your A-level course so far.

Can I:
- Say what I find interesting in books?
- Identify significant words in a passage?
- Make links between words, images, ideas and associations in a passage?
- Find significant words in a poem?
- Identify significant features in a passage of drama?
- Give reasons to support my opinions?
- Communicate these to others?
- Listen to their views?
- Modify my views in the light of the opinions of others?
- Work with others to agree on materials for presentation?
- Prepare and present materials for a defined audience?

This first part of the handbook has concentrated on encouraging students to find information and bring prior knowledge and experience to the A-level English classroom. It has sought to do this in a entitling way that will build students' confidence for the tasks ahead. It is probable that none of the activities we have outlined is new to the practising English teacher: what may be novel, however, is the manner in which we suggest that they are presented in the classroom, and it is this that is the essence of entitlement – the manner of presentation and the opportunities given for exercising autonomy offer the potential for the A-level English student to develop as an independent, self-motivating learner.

Section 2 of the handbook is a natural development of the ideas suggested in Section 1, applied now to the teaching programme that concentrates on study of the set texts. This section is the place for information and ideas on general matters that apply to close study in A-level English such as: procedures for studying the long text; working with settings; tracing themes; the analysis of character; approaching the question of narrators and narrative technique. Here also will be advice and activities concerning the writing of essays and coursework.

Section 2 will also serve as an extended record of progress during the course. Thus, although a student's personal study file will contain all the material relevant to a particular text, the handbook will be the place for the student to make periodic general reviews of progress on the course, covering the following matters:

Knowledge of texts
Understanding of texts
Reading skills
Research skills
Writing skills
Concentration in classes
Study time
Learning from others/group work
Enrichment activities
Progress
Additional comment
Future targets.

The third and final section of the handbook should take the form of a revision booklet to be given to students at an appropriate time before the final examinations. These materials could also be the subject of a study day, during which the advice is discussed with students and appropriate activities worked through. An example of the kind of information that Section 3 might contain is given here.

Personal Organization 1 – Using People

If you've been studying with a group, then you are all a resource for each other. Your teachers are also a resource. Use these resources in appropriate ways.

You might want to organize self-help groups with fellow students. You can consider either open-ended meetings, e.g.:

- 'Let's meet to talk about revision.'

or structured meetings, e.g.:

- 'Let's meet in Room 3.3 at 9.30 on Monday to look at our views on "Portrayal of women in Tender is the Night". Everyone to bring their own notes and be prepared to talk for 5 minutes.'

There's a time appropriate for each; negotiate an appropriate schedule with your group(s).

Teacher time – a precious and limited resource. Some possibilities may be:

- Short, personal time for you
- 'Pooling' time with a group for a specific topic
- An open-ended discussion with your teacher
- Input focused on a given area
- Spaced tutorial meetings during your revision period
- A block of time to: get you started, gee you up, consolidate just before the examination.

There may be other options, depending on your institution. However, it's important to discuss this with your teacher as soon as possible: he or she will want to advise you on the most appropriate formats and schedules for your group.

Personal Organization 2 – Using Resources

Have a folder for each of the texts on which you'll be examined. Start by working through this check-list for each of your texts.

Name of text:

What do I need to know?	Resources I can use	Gaps in my resources
whole or part the plot treatment of characters use of language settings themes structure appropriate quotation context and background critical views presentation on stage/film any others?	text text my notes, essays	

Your resources will include your notes, essays, handouts, diagrams, as well as relevant published material.
   If you identify gaps, how can you remedy this?

Other parts of this booklet might contain guidance on revision study patterns and timetables, the likely rubric of examination questions, and advice on how to proceed in the examination itself. As before, the emphasis should be on encouraging students to work together to articulate and then devise solutions to the problems that are likely to arise at this time in the course.

We have built our preliminary discussion of entitlement in the A-level English classroom around the notion of the handbook because this seems a natural focus for students to develop a sense of personal ownership of and involvement in the course. Such a source of personal information and recording will also provide the student with a basis for discussing her or his work with others concerned about progress and performance: teachers, parents, governors, fellow students and, of student with a basis for discussing her or his work with others concerned about progress and performance: teachers, parents, governors, fellow students and, of course, future employers or interviewers from higher education. In that sense, the handbook extends the idea of the Record of Achievement: but it is a considerable extension, since the handbook is more than simply a record. It develops the skills upon which it comments and, since it is the student's own compilation, reflects the degree of autonomy and independence gained through the course. As a final indication to students of the value of the handbook in the life of the English department in the school, they could be invited at the end of the course to make suggestions about what changes might be made to the handbook, and also to the course as a whole. Such a procedure would complete the process of taking students' views seriously and valuing their contribution to the English department's teaching and learning strategies.

General considerations

The scale of such a handbook and the part it will play in the total programme will be a matter for discussion within the English department and the school as a whole. Who will compile it? How will its production be resourced? How often will it be updated? Will it be issued in one piece or sequentially, as each element becomes appropriate? As a matter of policy, and with the greater financial freedom that schools and colleges now have, staff may find it advantageous to produce such materials to inform parents and governors about good practice in their institution.

CHAPTER 2

Developing Autonomy: The Teaching Challenge

Our consideration of entitlement in A-level English Literature has so far linked students' development of self-reliant learning habits with their gradual understanding and acquisition of the literary skills relevant to A-level. Self-reliance for the student of A-level English Literature thus consists of a number of features: being able to read observantly; being able to communicate one's views to others and to listen and respond to their opinions; being able to reach a consensus with others, or feel comfortable with a range of views, whichever is appropriate. If we are to enable students to take responsibility for forming and presenting their ideas in this way, we have suggested that they must be encouraged in habits of independent response from the start of the course, and the strategies outlined for the student handbook showed how this might be done. We now sketch out a programme that extends the entitlement approach into the set text components of the course. In terms of the skills of A-level literary study, we set out active learning strategies for close, careful reading and the analysis of texts; for going beyond the text into such research as is appropriate; for the expression of ideas in one's own language, appropriately illustrated from text; and for the presentation of these ideas to others in a logical and coherent manner, in both speech and writing. Paper 3 presents special problems for teachers wishing to embed the entitlement curriculum into their A-level syllabus; we discuss this issue in detail in the final part of this chapter.

Students can be resistant to the suggestion that they take responsibility for their learning. Feeling more secure with the teacher-as-expert, they are content to take the role of listeners and note-takers. Current pressures on teachers may encourage collusion in this model, but we argue that this is ultimately counter-productive. The teacher may be, in many respects, 'the expert' but, until students have expressed their understanding in their own words, neither they nor the teacher can say with any certainty what they have or haven't understood. Writing down what an expert says is no guarantee of understanding it. Moreover, as teachers, we frequently mistake what students will and will not find difficult, spending too much time on some aspects, insufficient on others. Unless students are involved from the first in articulating and clarifying their reactions, then misconceptions and misplaced emphases on their part do not surface until we find them in essays, by which time they have become part of the student's knowledge patterns and are much harder to change. Radical correction to written work is always disheartening for students: much better to clear up the areas of confusion at the earlier, opinion-forming, oral stage, through peer-group and directed class discussion.

Such observations are commonly expressed about teaching and learning at the pre-A-level stage, but the nature of the work at A-level and its demands on students and teachers can make it seem more problematic to carry on with these kinds of activities. To abandon them, however, is to stop trusting students as contributors to the learning and understanding process, and to confirm them in the view many of them have that they enter A-level work without skills or knowledge. The activities outlined and results demonstrated in the previous chapter show that this is far from the case: but the challenge is to continue to introduce, gradually and in a supportive way, activities that give students more and more confidence to trust their own judgements as they come to refine them through the development of appropriate skills. The teacher-as-expert does not disappear, but the expertise goes into a more facilitative mode, setting up learning situations rather than giving pre-digested information.

In this context, it is useful to make a distinction between 'knowing how' (having a skill that can be applied to other cases of the same thing, like knowing how to set about analysing poems) and 'knowing that' (being able to carry out an operation in a specific case, like being able to analyse *Anthem for Doomed Youth*). A genuinely entitling curriculum will seek to empower students with the former, and then give them opportunities to carry out these skills in particular cases. Thus, if we isolate certain elements, like character analysis, the tracing of themes, questions of narrators and narrative techniques, and their corresponding lines of enquiry, 'entitling' teaching strategies will give students these skills and the ability to adapt and apply them to any particular text they may be studying.

This point perhaps calls for further elaboration. It is quite customary, in the A-level teaching programme, to spend a good deal of time on the first text studied, so that skills of literary analysis can be explained to and practised by the students through their work on that particular text. The assumption is that students, having learned the skills from this text, will go on to 'transfer' them to subsequent texts. Doing character analysis in *Tess of the D'Urbervilles*, on this model, means learning about the characters in the novel and drawing inferences about the analysis of character that will be transferred without strain to the next text. Much here depends on the explicitness with which these techniques are made general – i.e., divested of any specific reference to *Tess of the D'Urbervilles* – and the students' own skill in generalizing for themselves from these specific examples. However, the student immersed in the complexities of Hardy's treatment of his characters, though likely to pick up points about Hardy's techniques, is less likely to make generalized points for her or himself about literary techniques of character presentation. And of course, if the teacher digresses too far into the general principles, then the immediate impact of Hardy's writing, and thus the flow of work on the novel, is likely to be disrupted.

We might ask, as teachers of literature, if we are making confusing demands on our students as learners by proceeding in this way. What we are asking students to do is to examine character in *Tess of the d'Urbervilles* and at the same time to draw from this work general inferences about strategies for undertaking literary analysis on any text. We are also expecting that they will keep the two types of knowledge separate, that is, that they will retain knowledge about the novel but also retain, separately and independently, a set of general rules about analysing any text. As proponents of an entitlement approach to the subject, we might ask if we are empowering our students as effectively as possible by going about things in this way.

It might be better to present our students with exercises and problems that will enable them to think through for themselves what the general aspects of literary enquiry are (character analysis, the tracing of themes, narrative techniques, etc.): as these are being teased out students can be asked to give illustrations from texts they are currently studying. The presentation of the activities makes it clear that these general elements are being addressed, so that the students distinguish from the beginning between general strategies and specific applications.

A further word may be in order before we proceed to the examples. For the hard-pressed teacher with a number of texts to cover, it may seem that we are asking for more time to be squeezed out of a teaching programme that is already overloaded. However, the gains that follow from this approach will in fact save time in the long run. If relevant skills are acquired, and consciously acquired, by students in the early stages of the course, the teacher is likely to be spending less time remaking the same points every time a new text is begun. It is worth considering a departmental approach: an English department could undertake jointly to build up resources along the lines we suggest, thus saving on materials-production time for individual teachers and providing within the department a continuing bank of resources for students who need to revise work on particular aspects.

Important features of the entitlement curriculum are embedded in the examples that follow. The proposed active learning methods involve individual and collaborative work. The activities are designed to develop students' conscious acquisition of analytical skills, in this case the skills necessary for literary analysis. Throughout, students are asked to comment on and assess their growing awareness of themselves as observant readers of literature and thus confirm their progress.

In these initial stages of the work, it is important that, though a group makes its presentation on only one task, it considers the other tasks too, albeit briefly. Students keyed up for a presentation of their own can feel less involved in the presentations of others: but learning how to listen and respond to these presentations is as important as giving their own. Not only is it at the heart of collaboration and the mutual building of confidence, it is a necessary part of developing response to text to be able to ask intelligent questions about the views of others. Once students can see the relevance of each other's tasks to the whole picture, then tasks do not need to be 'doubled up' in this way.

WORKING WITH SETTINGS

*Ros McCulloch, Lecturer in Education, Centre for English,
School of Education, University of Leicester*

> This guide will help you appreciate the importance of settings in literature. It suggests activities which will help you understand how writers use and establish setttings

Aims

This guide will help you:

- Consider how settings can influence action and characters
- Record important information about key events, characters and settings for any text
- Consider the techniques writers use to establish settings
- Consider how the cultural, historical and social implications of settings can influence narrative.

Use this box for important information - deadlines, length of your work, assessment, etc.

Activities

margin notes

Activity 1 : Settings and Scenarios

In this activity you will match a number of scenarios with settings and discuss the reasons for your choices.

Work with a partner to match each of the following scenarios with a setting (time and place) of your choice. Give reasons for your choice of setting.

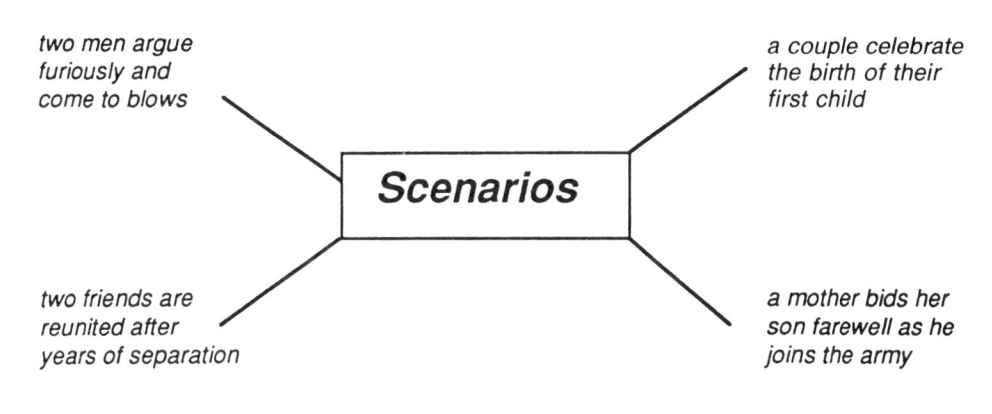

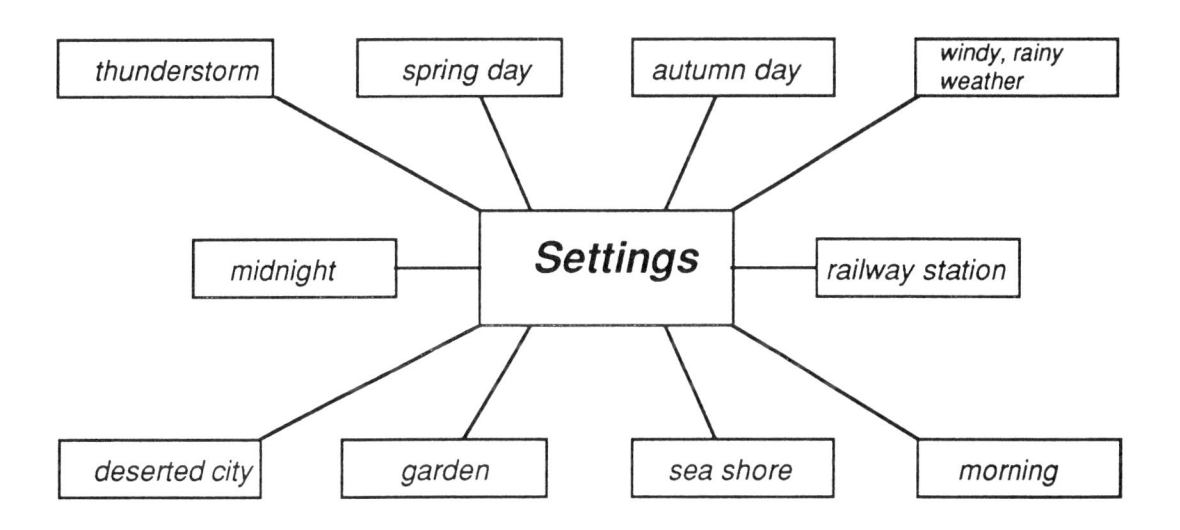

Scenarios

- two men argue furiously and come to blows
- a couple celebrate the birth of their first child
- two friends are reunited after years of separation
- a mother bids her son farewell as he joins the army

Settings

- thunderstorm
- spring day
- autumn day
- windy, rainy weather
- midnight
- railway station
- deserted city
- garden
- sea shore
- morning

When you have made your choices discuss them with other pairs. Make clear to each other your reasons for choosing either *contrasting* or *complementary* settings.

Make a class chart to show the various settings in which groups have placed each scenario and the reasons for their choices.

Scenario	Setting	Reasons
argument	thunderstorm	setting mirrors event
argument	summer morning	setting contrasts with event

Activity 2 : Finding your Bearings in a Text

margin notes

This activity will help you to see how the opening pages of a novel can develop your awareness of the meaning and direction of the text. Use the following ideas to help you make brief notes when you start to read a novel:

- Where is the story set? (country, urban/rural, inside/outdoors)
- When is the story set? (century, year, time of year, time of day)
- What are the features of the setting? (climate, poor/rich, etc.)

Activity 3 : Tracking the Novel

When you read a novel you need to:

- keep track of the key events and characters
- think about how the writer uses settings
- consider how the combination of key events, characters and settings affects the novel.

Use a grid to help you. For example

Tracking Key Events and Settings

Key events	Setting	What this adds to the novel	Evidence Quotations
Murder of important character	Dark house; midnight	Increases tension/ mystery	

Tracking Character and Settings

Key events	Setting	What this adds to the novel	Evidence Quotation
Moves from family home	From comfort to strange/alien city	Character's loneliness new challenge	

Use this method to help you monitor not only what happens but also where and when the action takes place. This will give you a clearer understanding of the way the writer uses settings.

Activity 4 : How Does a Writer Create Settings?

Select examples of poetry, prose and drama. List and compare how the writer has conveyed the setting. For example

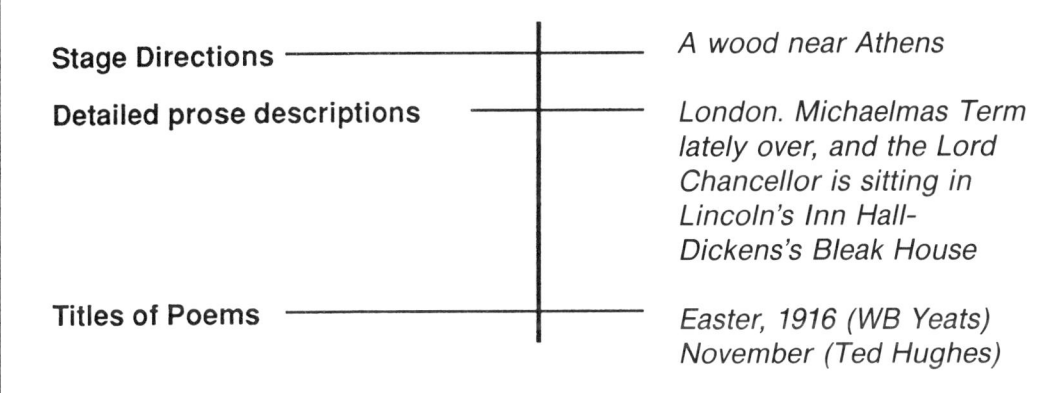

Stage Directions — *A wood near Athens*

Detailed prose descriptions — *London. Michaelmas Term lately over, and the Lord Chancellor is sitting in Lincoln's Inn Hall - Dickens's Bleak House*

Titles of Poems — *Easter, 1916 (WB Yeats) November (Ted Hughes)*

Activity 5 : Historical and Cultural Settings

This activity will help you to think about the relationship between the events in a text and historical time and place chosen by the writer.

A young man and woman are attracted to each other and contrive a meeting:
- In a society where marriage/courtship are arranged by parents
- In a society where this is the normal way for people to begin a relationship
- In a society where your partner is chosen for you by the state

- When girls couldn't leave a house alone or meet a man alone
- Each comes from a family who are sworn enemies

An old lady lives alone and keeps a cat:

- In a time when cats are carriers of a deadly virus
- In a society where able-bodied people take responsibility for the old & frail
- At a time when this was the mark of a witch
- In a time when cats are worshipped as having special powers

How might each story develop in each of the settings? List how the settings could influence what you think will happen. You might list these under headings such as:

- cultural
- historical
- social

In addition make a list of questions under these headings which you can use to help you find out how the cultural/historical/social settings of any text you are studying can influence what is likely to happen.

Conclusion

margin notes

Use what you have learnt from this guide to help you understand the importance of settings in any text you study. In particular you can use:

- The questions and chart from activities 2 and 3
- The way writers establish settings from activity 4
- The questions about the cultural/historical and social implications of any setting in activity 5

(Reproduced by kind permission of Network Educational Press.)

Developing group work and role-play skills for A-level English

We have argued that students' initial anxieties about the analysis of prose and poetry can be significantly allayed if A-level study begins with their own personal responses. Insofar as these are mediated through group work from the start, students are gaining the confidence to exchange ideas with each other. From this can be encouraged a shared responsibility for outcomes which, though initially modest (e.g., short presentations of findings), will give a basis for extension into more significant tasks (presentation of a whole topic, 'hot seating' and debating activities, dramatization of episodes). With this in mind, the activities presented above have had a dual focus: students were presented with opportunities to work out for themselves the various techniques of textual analysis, but in a way that involved discussion and cooperation, and the collation and presentation of ideas to their peers and teacher(s). Thus they were able to develop confidence in their views, take responsibility for the outcomes of their own work and, as importantly, respond to the work of others.

The kind of mutual confidence that can be built up by this kind of sharing can be used to advantage when students are first confronted by a more demanding text. In the following sequence of activities, small group discussion is extended into active role-playing to enable students to investigate for themselves the meanings within a difficult poem, in this case, *The Love Song of J. Alfred Prufrock*. Apart from initially setting the scene and reading the poem aloud to the class, the teacher simply gives instructions for the various stages of the activity: responsibility for findings and presentations rests entirely with the students.

Working on a difficult text:
The Love Song of J. Alfred Prufrock

1. Before students have sight of the poem, describe to them a man who is torn between passion and timidity, who wants to be heroic but who feels himself to be absurd, who cannot 'act' but plays for time, never quite daring to approach the woman who is the object of his desire. He becomes, instead, introspective and self-obsessed. One day he plans to visit her.

2. As a whole class activity, ask students to brainstorm the factors that might be stopping him.

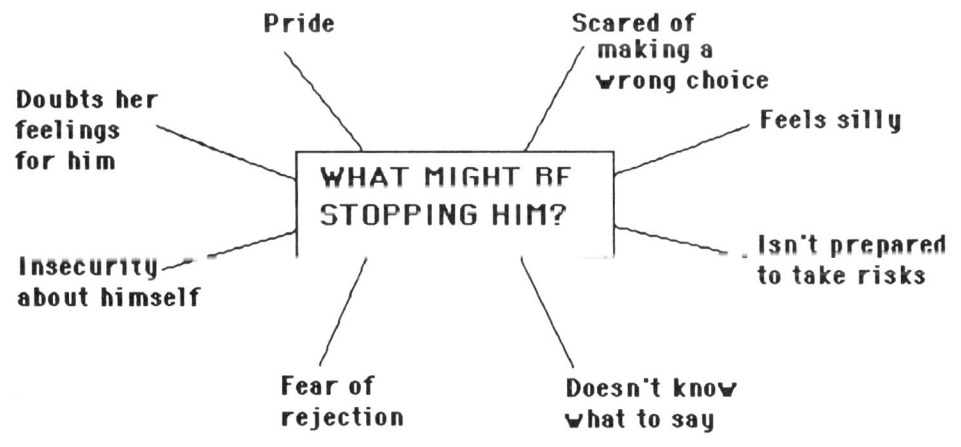

```
                    Pride        Scared of
                       \        / making a
        Doubts her      \      /  wrong choice
        feelings          \   /              Feels silly
        for him    \       \ /           /
                    ┌─────────────────┐
                    │  WHAT MIGHT BE  │
                    │  STOPPING HIM?  │
                    └─────────────────┘
        Insecurity /       / \            \  Isn't prepared
        about himself     /   \              to take risks
                         /     \
                   Fear of    Doesn't know
                   rejection  what to say
```

3. When this has been done, go on to tell the students that the man sets off, on foot. Ask them now to brainstorm what thoughts and feelings might run through his head as he makes his journey.

4. Summarize with the class the responses made so far.

Entitlement at A-level

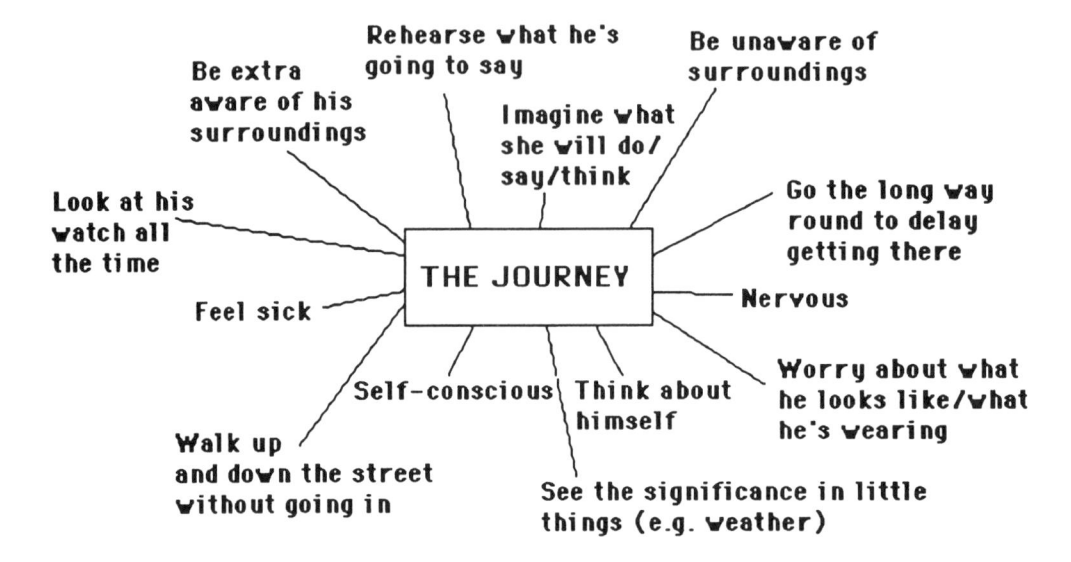

```
                    Rehearse what he's      Be unaware of
       Be extra     going to say            surroundings
       aware of his
       surroundings  Imagine what
                     she will do/
   Look at his       say/think
                                            Go the long way
   watch all                                round to delay
   the time                                 getting there
                     THE JOURNEY
         Feel sick                          Nervous

                  Self-conscious  Think about      Worry about what
                                  himself          he looks like/what
        Walk up                                    he's wearing
        and down the street
        without going in    See the significance in little
                            things (e.g. weather)
```

5. At this stage students listen to a complete reading of the poem, ideally given by the teacher.

6. Now ask students to begin to work with the poem. They should work in small groups of four or five, and start to identify, from the poem, Prufrock's feelings, thoughts and states of mind. Their list may look something like this:

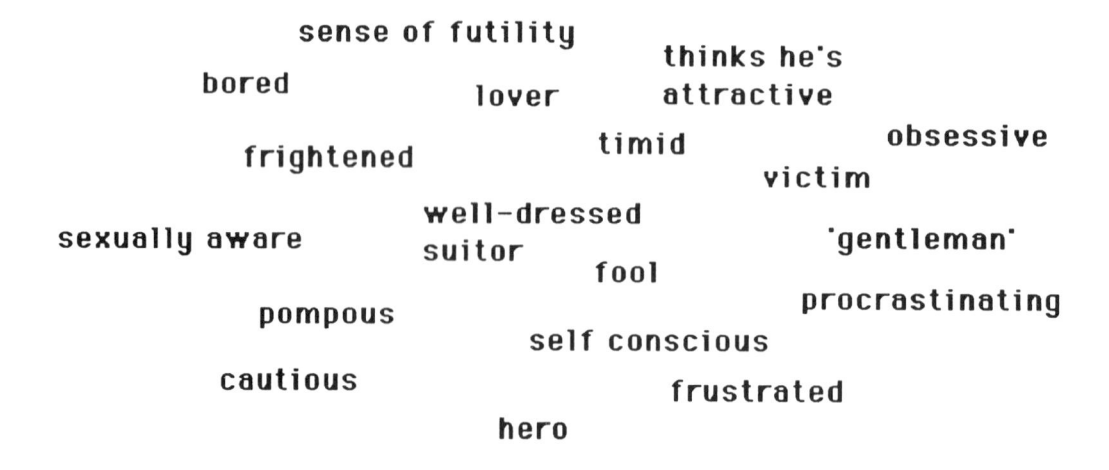

```
              sense of futility
                                       thinks he's
       bored                           attractive
                         lover
                                timid
            frightened                          obsessive
                                        victim
                      well-dressed
   sexually aware     suitor                    'gentleman'
                                fool
                                                procrastinating
              pompous
                          self conscious
           cautious
                                        frustrated
                         hero
```

7. Students should now match lines from the poem to the feelings, thoughts and states of mind that they listed in the earlier brainstorming exercises. They will pick out such words and phrases as 'Let us go', 'There will be time', 'Time to turn back', 'How should I presume?', 'Do I dare disturb the universe?', 'with a bald spot in the middle of my hair'.

Students should, at this stage, disregard allusions unfamiliar to them and simply concentrate on the 'story-line' of the poem.

8. There should now be class discussion of lines picked out and a collected list prepared, ideally for classroom display.

Comparing this approach to the poem with more traditional ones, where perhaps there has been preliminary explanation of the dense pattern of allusion in the poem and information given about Eliot's background, one is struck by how much more confident students are in their first responses to this difficult text. Working from the preliminary discussion of ideas which they generated themselves from their own understanding, and with which they can to some extent sympathize, students feel that the poem is brought nearer to them, and they are invited to have some ownership of Prufrock's emotions and ideas.

From these initial steps, group work can now be extended to investigate the poem's structure in a more complex and ambitious fashion. Students whose A-level work thus far has given them the confidence to share ideas, begin to feel that their own progress is part of a collaborative process with their peers. It is on this mutual trust that the following activities depend.

9. The class forms a circle, and individual students depict each stage of Prufrock's various states as he moves through the poem. For each 'freeze frame' moment, the student delivers an appropriate line. Thus, for example, student 1 represents Prufrock thinking himself rather attractive, looking smugly into a mirror, with the line 'My necktie rich and modest, but asserted by a simple pin'. Student 2 positions her or himself behind student 1, looking over her or his shoulder, dejected and perplexed, revealing Prufrock's insecurity about his physical appearance, with the line 'With a bald spot in the middle of my hair'.

10. As the picture builds up, the group is asked to consider which are the key/recurrent emotions experienced by Prufrock.

11. A group, or groups, of students are now asked to represent diagrammatically the psychological changes which Prufrock undergoes through the poem by selecting quotations and arranging them on a large sheet of paper in order to help understand the relationship between Prufrock's desire and his inability to act.

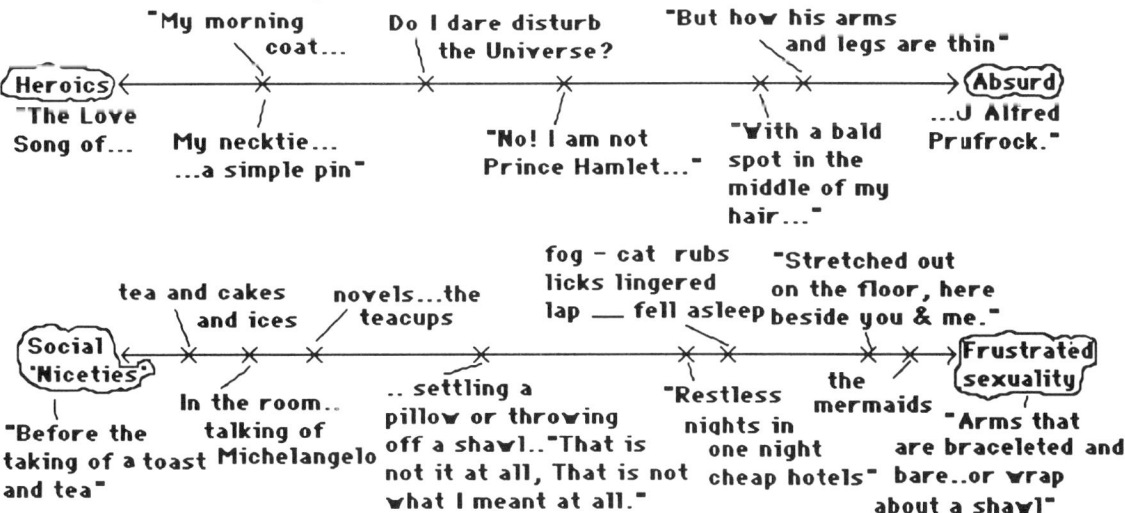

12. Remaining group(s) of students are asked to draw up a mapping continuum, by noting the extremes of character and mood displayed by Prufrock, placing them at each end of a continuum, and selecting up to five key moments or phrases from the poem to mark on the continuum.

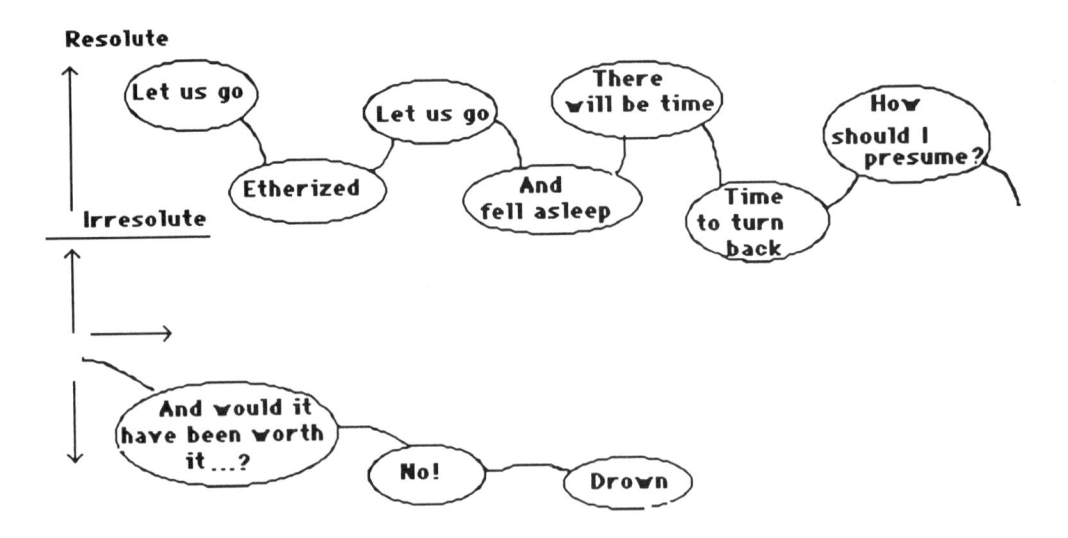

Resolute

- Let us go
- Etherized
- Let us go
- And fell asleep
- There will be time
- Time to turn back
- How should I presume?

Irresolute

- And would it have been worth it ...?
- No!
- Drown

13. The various groups now share their findings, and a summary version of each exercise is drawn up for classroom display.

14. Students are now asked to work in similar 'role play' fashion on the 'landscapes' of the poem. Ask students to develop any of the scenes that are shown in the poem, working in small groups e.g., the 'seedy' side of society (the prostitute, the couple embracing, the voice out of an open window, the drunkard, etc.) and the 'polite society' of afternoon tea and chit-chat. Again, frozen images may be constructed out of which snatches of conversation and speech from the poem can be heard.

15. Small 'scenarios' of these moments can be constructed in visual form, using cut-out pictures, with appropriate lines written in: again this should be part of the classroom display.

16. After this is done there is class discussion of the effects of capturing these 'moments' of the poem clearly, how this relates to Prufrock's momentary vision and memories, and thus to the significance of 'the moment' in the poem.

We have drawn upon the ideas of the entitlement curriculum to suggest approaches to a complex text. Students are likely to be more confident in their responses to a poem of this complexity if they are given opportunities to reflect upon their own experiences and previous reading. In this way they are anticipating, and empathizing with, the emotions, states of mind and/or events which are recreated in the poem. Such preparatory work can overcome much of the nervousness with which students approach a poem as initially daunting as this one, and with a grasp of story-line, shifting moods and the various landscapes of the poem, they feel that they have made significant progress.

The students' knowledge base

The methods we have discussed above work from the student's own knowledge base, and we have purposely left until now the tricky question of the poem's allusions. This is part of the general question of the knowledge that students bring to the study of English Literature. This, many teachers agree, is radically different from the classical, Christian background upon which so much of English Literature draws. In the poem we have been considering, discussion of the allusions of the poem should be left to the end, since we feel that students should not be asked to consider these until they have an adequate grasp of its thoughts and ideas as they have been investigated above. To proceed in any other way, for example to introduce the difficult allusions and references first, is to risk 'losing' the students at once, as they are likely to be intimidated by the weight of this (for many) unfamiliar information. A key aim of entitlement, empowering the student from the first with confidence to start from her or his own resources, is lost.

Nonetheless, students are still 'entitled' to have access to that information, better still, to have opportunities to find it out for themselves, and so the question of the knowledge base needs further discussion. Returning to the distinction between 'knowing how' and 'knowing that' already mentioned, what is important is that students have the skills necessary to find information, ('knowing how') so that, if research is required on a particular text, ('knowing that') they know where to look, how to make the most effective use of their time, both individually and in groups, and how to integrate their findings into the text.

In the case of the particular text, however, the teacher's decision on how much of this kind of activity should be pursued is a pragmatic one. If a text of the complexity of *The Love Song of J. Alfred Prufrock* is the only poem of Eliot's which the students will be studying, then it would be counter-productive to organize, say, a series of small research projects for students to investigate the classical, Christian and Shakespearean allusions in the poem. The amount of time this would need would far outweigh the time given to those activities designed to give students confidence in handling the poem's 'story-line', and they may well be as intimidated as ever by the long complex poem. It might be better under these circumstances for the teacher to give short, rather understated glosses on the allusions, stressing all the time that they serve to enrich the meaning that students have already discovered for themselves, rather than make any radical changes to meanings and significances.

However, if T.S. Eliot is a major writer for study, it will be appropriate to approach the question of the knowledge base in a different way. An entitling approach will look for ways to allow students to gain as much of this information for themselves as possible. The teacher may be anxious about constraints of time, but careful scheduling can overcome this. As will be shown in the following chapter, in the example of *The Background to Victorian Literature*, appropriate topic areas can be outlined, and study time for students to investigate them can be organized, within the framework of the English timetable. Students can then present their findings to their peers so that the whole class has the necessary background knowledge. This text-specific, sharply-focused approach is probably more useful for students than any pre-course general introduction to English Literature, the relevance of which they will not immediately see and which they will thus be unlikely to remember. Information sought for particular purposes and immediately applied to the text in question in a way that makes sense to the students, on the other hand, is more likely to be retained and used.

Extending the knowledge base: introduction to research methods

When students are required to undertake research as part of the study of their A-level texts, it is important that they should feel confident that they can find out information for themselves. First steps are, of course, book-searching techniques, and the skills of skimming and scanning. All of this can be done through group work, with the added incentive that groups must divide the activities if the task is to be completed in time. The total time for the following exercise should be 1 hour 30 minutes, of which the first 30 minutes is tutor input. Students have an hour to answer the questions.

It is better for this activity that the tutor is not a literature specialist, since part of the aim of the session is to show students that the range of techniques with which they are being asked to work are the general aspects of book searching.

The tutor should remind students at the start of the session of the range of reading and searching techniques and provide short examples of, for example, skimming, scanning, contents search and index search. Through some further examples and discussion, the tutor indicates the place of these techniques in preliminary literature research. Students are then given the research task sheet. The book chosen to illustrate the activity in this case is *Tender is the Night* (F. Scott Fitzgerald); any book which students are currently studying would be suitable.

Students have an hour to complete the tasks, and they need to decide how they will organize themselves (e.g., into sub-groups with allocated tasks, agreed times, and opportunity for sharing findings, etc.). After students have completed the tasks, there should be an opportunity to discuss the procedures carried out, the skills practised, any difficulties that arose, and what hey felt was learned from the activity.

Topics for research methods in Literature

You have an hour to work through the questions on this sheet. However, do not answer the topics – simply work out which books, and where appropriate which pages, you would use to answer the topics.

1. Indicate how events and people in Fitzgerald's own life furnished him with material for *Tender is the Night*.

2. In what ways do you find the information in Fitzgerald's 'Notes' helpful for your understanding of the novel?
3. Analyse the character of Dick Diver in *Tender is the Night*.
4. Discuss the significance of Keats's *Ode to a Nightingale* for Fitzgerald's *Tender is the Night*.
5. Outline attitudes towards women as they are exemplified in *Tender is the Night*.

Books available for you to consult:
Arthur Mizener: *Scott Fitzgerald and his World* (Thames and Hudson, 1972)
Arthur Mizener: *The Far Side of Paradise* (Heinemann, 1969)
Marvin Lattwood: *Tender is the Night: Essays in Criticism* (Indiana University Press, 1969)
Milton Stern: *The Golden Moment: The Novels of F. Scott Fitzgerald* (University of Illinois, 1970)
Avare LeVot: *F. Scott Fitzgerald: A Biography* (Allen Lane, 1983).

Written presentations

The activities that we have described depend on individual contributions made during oral work in small group settings. We turn now to the written demands of the A-level English Literature paper. Systematic development of students' oral skills as part of their entitlement may seem an innovative addition to regular classroom work, but the demands of the essay and the strain this imposes on students have always been part of the concern of English teachers. Clearly it is part of the students' entitlement that they be helped to overcome their fears about essay writing. Additionally, a high level of written communication skills is of course part of every student's entitlement as a preparation for later life.

GCSE coursework practice has undoubtedly helped students to become accustomed to drafting and re-drafting their work and to recognize that the production of a thoughtful piece of writing takes time, patience and concentrated planning. However, the extra requirements of A-level can make the task seem very daunting: questions demand complex responses couched in more formal language with the use of technical vocabulary; additionally, students may be required to consult a range of critical texts.

The methods we have suggested in this chapter for collaborative work as a way to increase students' confidence can be used successfully in developing written work. First, written work should build on the activities already outlined for small group discussion leading to short presentations. When students have become confident about expressing their ideas to each other, and refining them through group discussion and oral presentation, (where the role of written work is to provide notes for the presentation) then they will be happier about making the transition to more formal written forms of expression. Second, these methods can also focus on the essay-writing task itself. Students working together to clarify the various strands of A-level essay writing can learn from each other and mutually gain confidence. The following series of activities sets out a programme for this work.

WRITING ESSAYS AT A LEVEL

Cheryl McLeod, The Robert Symth School, Market Harborough

> This guide gives you advice on how to prepare, plan and write A Level essays. Use it throughout your A Level studies to help you write successful essays.

Aims

margin notes

This guide will help you to:

- Understand what an essay title requires
- Collect material for your essay
- Plan the structure of your essay
- Write your introductory and concluding paragraphs
- Structure your main paragraphs
- Set out quotations
- Write in the appropriate style

Use this box for important information - deadlines, length of work, assessment, etc.

Resources

- Texts you are studying

- Notes on your texts
- A copy of your syllabus
- Sample essay questions
- Sample answers
- Examiners' reports
- Critical essays
- Fellow students
- Teachers and tutors

You, your group or your teacher may find other resources. List them in this box.

Activities

margin notes

Activity 1 : Understanding Essay Titles

It is important to develop the ability to recognise precisely what an assignment requires. This activity suggests how to do this. Read every part of your essay title very carefully. Break it down into separate components.

- Look for *key words*: these are the words which tell you what you will have to do.

- Look for the *focus*: who or what are you going to be writing about?

- Look for the *theme*: this is the topic you will explore.

Example: *How far are Romeo and Juliet responsible for what happens to them?*

- The *key words* in this title are *how far.*

- The question *focuses* on Romeo and Juliet.

- The *theme* to explore is their responsibility for their fate.

The title could be set out like the following table. (The table also includes examples of other essay titles.)

Key Words	Meaning	Focus	Theme
How far....	to what extent	Romeo, Juliet	Responsible for fate
Compare and contrast....			
Discuss the implications of...			
In what ways....			

margin notes

Collect essay titles for all/any of your set texts. Use the chart to help you break these titles down into their different components. The chart includes some frequently used key words to start you off, but you will find others in past papers.

Activity 2 : Collecting Material for your Essay (1) - The Process

When you have been given an essay title, identify its key words, focus and themes. Jot down some initial ideas for each component.

After you have outlined what the essay requires you need to collect relevant material. This might involve you in some/all of the following:

- re-reading relevant parts of the text(s)

- discussing the question with other students

- re-reading your notes, printed handouts and any other relevant information

- using a booklist to help you with further research

Try to do the following as you form your opinions about the question:

- think in advance of your writing

- try not to be overwhelmed by the material. There will be a lot of it.

- keep a separate list of the main points you will want to make

- annotate material to help you remember which point you may use it for

- remember, there is no single right answer. You will be marked on your argument and evidence

margin notes

Activity 2 : Collecting Material for your Essay (2) - An Example

This activity shows you an example of how to collect material for an essay. Follow the process outlined in Activity 2(1). Read it carefully. Note its key features and stages. Try to apply it to an essay you are working on.

Title: *How far are Romeo and Juliet responsible for what happens to them?*

(i) **Use the Key Words - Focus - Theme process**

Key Words	-	*How far*
	-	*totally? partly? not at all?*
	-	*Who or what else could be responsible?*
Focus	-	*Romeo and Juliet*
	-	*What do they do?*
	-	*What is done to them?*
Theme	-	*responsible for their own fate*
	-	*Judge the impact of what they do and of what happens to them.*

Entitlement at A-level

(ii) **Collecting material**

Start	-	Read text
Analyse	-	Characters of Romeo and Juliet
List	-	Their own weaknesses
		Effect on them of other characters
		Strokes of fate and destiny
		Examples of chance and coincidence

(iii) **Select relevant illustrations**

What they say/quotations
What they do
What others say about them
How external events affect them

(iv) **Critical Reflection**

Judge the evidence
Form your opinion
Come to your conclusion

margin notes

Activity 3 : Planning and Writing your Essay - The Structure

Here are a few "Do's" and "Don'ts" you should consider when planning your essay:

Don't		Do
Don't repeat the question. Don't give your conclusion here.	**Introduction**	Do say what you intend to do. Do define the terms of the question.
Don't jump from one point to another. Don't make a statement without proof	**Main Body**	Do set our points in logical order. Use paragraphs. Do support points by - example, illustration, quotation. Do add comments to explain the significance of your evidence.
Don't make a statement without proof	**Conclusion**	Do state your points strongly. Answer the question.

Review and read through.
Ask yourself: Are my points presented logically?
Did I answer the question?

Make any necessary amendments to your plan.

Activity 4 : Tracking and Planning the Structure of an Essay

This activity shows you how to use the work of past students to help you see how essays can be structured.

Collect examples of past A Level essays from your tutor. Read them and produce a chart which shows how they were planned. Use the following headings:

- introduction
- main body
- conclusion

Decide how clearly the writers of the essays you have followed use the guidance in this guide. You could even grade the essays on a A - U scale for their clarity of organisation.

margin notes

Activity 5 : Introducing and Concluding your Essays

You will find it helpful to spend some time thinking about how you could plan an essay's structure. Use the following ideas to help you.

Small group activity

- Select an essay title relevant to your text
- Decide the main points that the answer should contain (use key word - focus - theme to help you.)

- Put the main points in order. Discuss and justify the order you select.
- Write the introductory and concluding paragraphs to your essay. Read them out to the rest of your group. Discuss everyone's version.

Decide who wrote the most effective paragraphs. Be clear about the reasons for this.

Activity 6 : Main body paragraphs and using quotations from the text

This activity outlines the main points to remember when writing paragraphs in the main body of your essay and suggests when to use quotations.

Starting and concluding the paragraphs

Bègin your main body paragraphs which a sentence which states its purpose clearly.

Conclude these paragraphs by stating how your argument relates to the essay title.

Using Quotations

Example 1 : Context - quote - comment

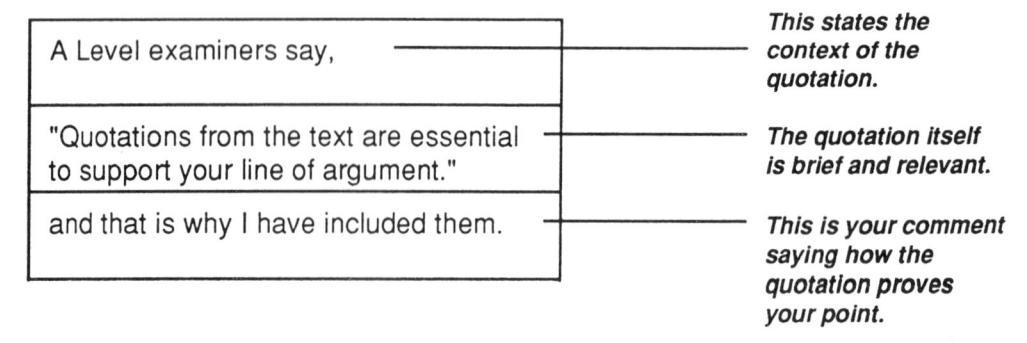

A Level examiners say,	*This states the context of the quotation.*
"Quotations from the text are essential to support your line of argument."	*The quotation itself is brief and relevant.*
and that is why I have included them.	*This is your comment saying how the quotation proves your point.*

Always use the context - quote - comment sequence.

margin notes

Example 2 : How to display longer quotations

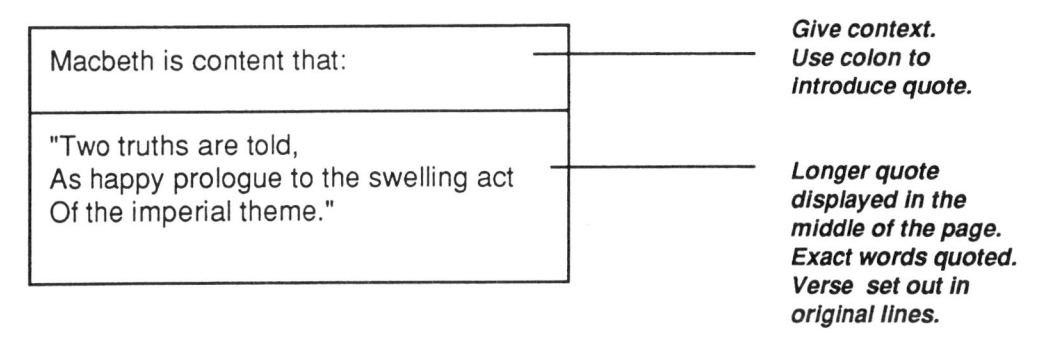

Macbeth is content that:

——————— *Give context. Use colon to introduce quote.*

"Two truths are told, As happy prologue to the swelling act Of the imperial theme."

——————— *Longer quote displayed in the middle of the page. Exact words quoted. Verse set out in original lines.*

Example 3 : How to set out shorter quotations

Lady Macbeth admonishes her husband declaring, "The sleeping and the dead/Are but pictures."

Note:

- The context is stated

- Use a comma to introduce shorter quotations. They are not displayed. Instead integrate them into your sentence.

- Use a slash followed by a capital letter to show where a new line of verse begins in the original text.

Activity 7   Using a clear prose style

Read through the following points. If you follow them you will be well on the way to writing successful essays.

- Think before you write

- Use a straightforward sentence structure

- Avoid using long and involved sentences

- Choose the exact vocabulary you need

- Avoid repetition and don't be long winded

- Construct your paragraphs carefully

- Never point out a literary device without commenting on its effect
- Know your linguistic faults: learn from previous corrections
- Read through your completed essay for sense and accuracy
- Avoid wholesale copying of critics *(plagiarism)*

Conclusion

This guide contains a lot of information. You will probably find it is better not to try to take it all in at once. Use it in "bite-sized" chunks. Refer to it throughout your A Level studies and it will provide ongoing support for essay writing.

Additional Notes

(Reproduced by kind permission of Network Educational Press)

The practical criticism paper: constraints

This chapter has outlined ways in which students' entitlement may be embedded within the day-to-day work of the A-level English classroom, without in any way compromising the rigour of the subject or the demands of the traditional syllabus. In that way we have shown that A-level English Literature is a subject that lends itself readily to the implementation of the entitlement curriculum. However, it must be acknowledged that there is a component of the A-level syllabus and assessment procedures which is less than fully entitling for many students. We refer, of course, to the unseen practical criticism paper, which continues to be a feature of assessment procedures on even the most innovative syllabuses.

It is cruelly ironic that an element of the English Literature examination which was introduced in part for egalitarian motives should, 40 years later, have become the major disentitling feature of the syllabus. The practical criticism paper has today become the most serious obstacle to successful examination performance for a significant number of students of A-level English Literature. There is plentiful evidence available during the past 20 years of students' lack of confidence about the unseen examination at A-level. Peet and Robinson argued in 1977 that 'poor performance in the Unseen is the greatest single reason for failure among Advanced level candidates' (p. xii). Since then, annual breakdowns of marks achieved on the three English papers consistently reveal the failure of many students to perform as well on the unseen examination as on their set texts.

Explanation for candidates' insecurity in this examination can be found partly in cultural changes in British society and partly in the changes which have taken place in English 11–16 since the 1960s. In the early years after the war, candidates taking A-level English Literature came from a minority aspiring to university, whose version of English in schools was likely to be based upon Latin and Greek, and whose background knowledge of Christian beliefs was secure. For the small proportion of these candidates who were from lower middle-class backgrounds, an unseen practical criticism paper could offer opportunities to demonstrate personal sensitivity to literature: this, supporters of the innovation thought, would offset classroom advantages which candidates from more privileged school backgrounds might have had.

Today's far larger A-level population has experienced a very different cultural ambience: many come from a non-Christian tradition anyway, and all of them are exposed to a far greater extent than before to the influences of popular culture. Consequently, they are less well-equipped than their predecessors to recognize the historical, Christian and classical allusions likely to underpin much of the meaning of their unseen passages, especially the poems. Teachers of A-level Literature are concerned that candidates from ethnic minorities and from backgrounds with less of an emphasis on print culture may be specially disadvantaged when confronted with unseen passages from literature which are partly dependent on confident familiarity with culturally-specific allusions.

Changes in the teaching of English have contributed to these problems. During the 1960s and 1970s, 'progressive' English and Humanities were introduced to enliven the earlier 'classical' version of the subject. As well as reducing emphasis on the historical and cultural knowledge base of English Literature, these innovations re-directed attention away from knowledge about the technicalities of literary analysis, to pupils' personal responses to literature and their awareness of its relationship to social issues. Nonetheless, the criticism paper continues to demand from candidates a high level of ability to write intelligently about how technicalities feature in the unseen poetry and prose extracts.

Candidates are thus doubly disadvantaged in this examination, which expects the integration of the experience of literature, first with knowledge about cultural references, and second with the craft of writing. Taking the former problem first, it will be evident that the teacher of English, however conscientious, can go only a small way towards preparing her or his candidates for the potential range of references in the extracts of a paper which draws upon the literature of any century. The active learning strategies that we have proposed in this book can help in the limited sense that they can increase students' confidence and willingness to trust their own judgement, which will give them less of a feeling of terror before the paper. But whilst the A-level English Literature examination remains unreformed there is no doubt that, for some students, unfamiliarity with specific cultural references will continue to disadvantage them in this paper.

The practical criticism paper: opportunities

Where active learning strategies can help, however, is in the area of knowledge about the craft of writing. Much of the dissatisfaction expressed by the examiners does in fact centre on this aspect of candidates' response. In 1979, the AEB Examiners' Report complained:

> Most candidates wrote very badly, and many who did so seemed far from unintelligent. Worthy, caring candidates after worthy caring candidates simply did not know how to set about the Practical Criticism of short literary texts.

In 1981 similar dissatisfaction was expressed in the JMB Examiners' Report:

> There was, in some cases, simply not enough attention paid to the experience of the poem, to its tone, mood and feeling, which need to be responded to if the poem is to be fully understood and appreciated. Failure to do this led to failure to grasp the meaning, leading to an inability to maintain a consistent and logical argument.

Ten years later, the same concerns are being expressed by JMB Examiners:

> Another characteristic of answers in which candidates seemed to be evading an engagement with meaning was their concern with sound effects. There was a tedious recitation of 'examples of assonance and alliteration.' When an attempt was made to explain the effect of these devices the explanation was often extremely fanciful.
>
> Most of the comments on verse movement were quite empty. There were few valid comments on verse form; more frequently offered were syllable counts and alphabetical representations of rhyme schemes.
>
> As always, the invitation to consider style was generally declined. Most of those who accepted the invitation did not really comment on style, but

Developing Autonomy: The Teaching Challenge 51

Table 2.1 Suggested questions for students to use in classroom discussions of poetry

QUESTIONS TO ASK YOURSELF

READING POEMS

Title/s	Speaker/s and audiences	Settings	Time/s	Attitude/s	Language
What do the key words in the title bring to mind?	Who is the speaker? It is usually, but not always, the poet.	Where is the poem set? Is the setting the same throughout?	When does the experience take place? Is it the same time throughout?	What is the poet's attitude towards the subject of the poem? Does it change during the course of the poem?	Which words/phrases interest or impress you? Are there any words which look, feel or sound like the experience being described?
Could they, or the whole title, have more than one meaning?	Who is the poet addressing, him/herself, us, a listener inside or outside the poem?	Does it change inside or between verses or sections of the poem?	Does the time change inside or between verses or sections of the poem?	Does he/she resolve questions which are raised?	Are there any comparisons which help you to imagine the experience?
Do you need to check the meaning of any words?		If so, how does the setting change and why?	If so, how does the time change and why?	Do any contradictions or problems remain?	Are there any striking arrangements such as lists or repetitions which relate to the poet's subject?

WHAT IS THE POEM ABOUT?

simply repeated their account of the subject matter (JMB Examiners' Report, 1991).

The strategies that we have been proposing in this chapter can go a considerable way towards helping students to cope with this feature of Paper 3. The active learning methods we have described encourage students both to feel confident about engaging personally with the texts, and to blend this engagement with an appreciation of how technical features contribute to meaning. This can be done in a number of ways: for example, students can be encouraged to bring to unseen passages a set of questions which will yield aspects of the meaning to them. The template shown in Table 2.1 would be an appropriate model for students to use in their classroom discussions of poetry. Students encouraged to interrogate the text in this way during their experience of poetry on their A-level course will, it is hoped, be able to ask similar questions of the poem(s) in their practical criticism paper.

In these ways we hope that some of the constraints experienced by A-level English Literature students and their teachers might be overcome, with a consequent beneficial effect on examination results.

References

AEB (1979) *Examiners' Report*, Guildford: AEB.
JMB (1981) *Examiners' Report*, Manchester: JMB.
JMB (1991) *Examiners' Report in English*, Manchester: JMB.
McCulloch, R. (Ed.) (in press) *A-level English Literature*, Stafford: Network Educational Press.
McCulloch, R. (ed.) (1991) *A-level English*, Leicestershire Post-16 Development Programme, Leicestershire LEA.
Peet, M. and Robinson, D. (1977) *The Critical Examination*, Oxford: Pergamon Press.

CHAPTER 3

The Flexible Learning Classroom

We have thus far discussed the skills and competences that are involved in entitlement, and shown how these might be introduced into teaching and learning practices in the A-level English classroom. It will have become clear that there are organizational as well as resource implications here. For departments wishing to make these innovations, the Flexible Learning Framework is a recent initiative that offers practical guidance. The aims of Flexible Learning, entirely consonant with those of entitlement, are: 'to meet the learning needs of students as individuals and in groups through the flexible management and use of a range of learning activities, environments and resources', and 'to give the student increasing responsibility for her/his learning within a framework of appropriate support' (TA, 1989).

Flexible Learning came to prominence in post-16 curriculum development through the support of TVEI and the Employment Department. The earlier version of this strategy, 'Supported Self Study', had been attractive to LEAs wishing to maintain students' access to a full range of A-level subjects during a period of falling rolls. However, as this strategy has been developed, its considerable potential for revitalizing teaching and learning in the classroom has been recognized (Waterhouse 1983, 1990, etc.). Indeed, TVEI Extension asked LEAs to consider flexible teaching and learning styles in their plans for the 16–18 phase from 1988, and between 1989 and 1991 various regional Flexible Learning projects were established. In 1991 the Employment Department published the Flexible Learning Framework and set a target of embedding student-centred learning into the 14–19 curriculum by 1993. Indeed as Whiteside remarks, 'It (Flexible Learning) has become the "best word" of the early 1990s replacing "enterprise" in its value and appeal' (Whiteside *et al.*, 1992. p. 17).

Further examination of the concept of Flexible Learning shows just how closely it conforms to the aims of entitlement which we have been discussing. Students working in a Flexible Learning format are involved in such matters as: defining roles and responsibilities within their group, using a range of resources, discussing information, and collating and presenting their findings. The activities should be open-ended in nature, allow space for a variety of responses according to ability and interest, and give opportunities for students to develop their own approaches through the insights they gain into their own learning. The emphasis on student responsibility for managing the activities means that the teacher is able to target help in appropriate ways at appropriate times to particular students. Sometimes these will be teaching needs, where a group has difficulty with the text; sometimes the teacher's role will be facilitative, helping the group to work as a cooperative unit, negotiate its timetable and plan its presentation.

Similar changes in student behaviour from the passive to the active mode were outlined in detail in previous chapters in our discussion of moves from didactic teaching styles to those which gradually give more and more responsibility to the student. In what follows we show how a school in Leicestershire, wishing to modify its A-level English teaching by introducing entitlement skills and competences, successfully used the organizational ideas suggested by the Flexible Learning Framework to introduce change. For both teachers and students involved the experience has been a rewarding one.

Robert Smyth School (Market Harborough, Leicestershire): a case study

Staff at this school already had considerable experience of and enthusiasm for student-centred approaches as a result of its participation in the GCSE Leicestershire Modular Framework. They were encouraged by an evaluation (in 1990) which had shown that students appreciated opportunities to have some choice about the structure and planning of their assignments, and to engage afterwards in self-assessment. The English staff's interest in extending these ideas to A-level English Literature took its initial impetus from Leicestershire LEA's A-level Enhancement Project (ALEP, 1989). In particular they were influenced by the work of the A-level English Literature team, whose book was felt to be in tune with the department's own thinking. Further encouragement came from the LEA's involvement in Flexible Learning, the aims of which, as we have already seen, are entirely consonant with those of Entitlement.

English department staff began by stating the outcomes they hoped for from the programme:

- more help for sixth-form staff in coping with recent and impending curriculum changes
- increased collaboration with colleagues
- more effective use of teaching time to allow monitoring, review and recording of individual student's progress
- wider choice of teaching method; a greater variety of learning activities and a wider range of options for managing scarce resources
- a move away from the controller/director role in the classroom for staff, to one in which staff were seen as facilitators of student learning.
(Hardy, 1990)

The sixth form at Robert Smyth numbered 331 students, 114 in the lower sixth and 129 in the upper sixth. There are 11 classes and 8 members of staff, all full-time, all committed to the project. Classrooms are spacious and there is a recently completed, well-equipped sixth form centre. The school follows the Leicester syllabus, a JMB syllabus which is composed of a consortium of local schools, and contains a substantial coursework component.

Tutoring arrangements

Staff went on to consider the implications of mounting a programme to introduce changed teaching styles: appropriate teaching materials would have to be produced, students would have to be inducted into the use of these materials, and the staff-student relationship, particularly the new, expanded tutoring role would need to be prepared for. To cater for this a booklet, 'Guidance for Tutors' was produced, and the following programme adopted.

Each class following the programme is divided into groups, and each group is assigned a task or tasks. The teacher has, at stated times, a tutorial with each group, while the others work alone, in the classroom, in the Resource Centre, or in the sixth form study area. Since it is difficult to handle more than four groups and maintain supportive continuity, the size of the groups depended on the number in the class. (Between five and eight is generally reckoned to be an appropriate number – big enough to be intellectually stimulating and socially supportive, small enough for each member to feel important and responsible; the staff opted for this pattern.) The question of selection of groups was discussed: whether these groups would be self-chosen or chosen by the teacher; composed on the basis of friendship, mixed ability, gender, temperament, styles of working and thinking, or random choice. These are all matters for the individual teacher or school to decide.

Staff felt it would be advisable to vary the composition of groups throughout the year as the class moved from one set of tasks to another, or from one text to another. That way, the inevitable imperfections of any one grouping would be off-set; as importantly, students would become accustomed to working with a variety of different colleagues, and would thus develop their own style of cooperation and adaptation, rather than become set in the ways of a particular group dynamic.

As sixth form students become used to working in this style, it is sufficient to have one intensive tutorial with each group every one or two weeks. When a group is not being tutored, it continues with its tasks.

Tutoring roles for this kind of learning vary according to the stage the group has reached in its work, but will include:

- helping groups and individuals within groups to set clear objectives for each learning task
- helping groups and individuals to make useful work plans
- encouraging active participation of group members and an atmosphere of mutual support
- helping groups to work effectively as a team during tutorial
- supporting groups with information and ideas about resources
- setting an example of a disciplined intellectual approach to the work

Teaching materials

Robert Smyth staff decided to concentrate in the first instance on producing materials and activities for their students, based on their A-level syllabus texts. This INSET work was carried out during the spring and summer terms of 1991, the English department working with one of the authors of this book to produce learning materials on a number of texts. Devising appropriate tasks is as difficult as gauging the tone when producing materials for this work. These tasks must be stimulating enough to draw students in and motivate them to engage in the work, but demanding and extensive enough to occupy them for the length of time they will be functioning as self-supporting groups, between tutorials. Examples of typical materials are given at the end of this chapter; in what follows now we report on the success of this work with students and teachers.

Student responses and the entitlement curriculum

Entitlement competences are at the forefront of the learning activities, and the students' own responses to a monitoring questionnaire show that the materials successfully developed these: 'improvements in presentation skills' and the 'development of research skills' headed their list; with 'planning skills', 'taking responsibility for their own learning' and 'time management' coming next. The extent to which students had internalized the vocabulary of autonomous learning and a consciousness of themselves as learners is shown by their own comments:

> [The pack] seems a little simple and too easy for second year sixth.
> (Another student, with perhaps greater insight, offered this):
> [Although] rather basic, students from either year could do it with different levels of work.
> Anybody could have done at least one task from the pack.
> The pack allowed individual's skills to come through so that you could present the information in a way that each student could feel comfortable with their best work.
> Skills already developed in previous years could be put into practice again. ... It was fun working together instead of alone.
> We were allowed to think for ourselves, which makes a change from the usual [teaching] methods.

Though most students expressed satisfaction with their final presentation, they showed an ability to be quite critical and self-critical:

> I was pleased with my work until I saw what some of the others had achieved; then I realized that there were several ways I could have improved my own presentation.
> With better equipment we could make the video more professional but I think the content was quite good.

Next time I would use the time more efficiently, do more research and spend more time practising the talk.

Staff responses

Further support for our claim that the materials developed students' abilities and their capacity to comment on these in a detached, objective way comes from the staff reports on the students' learning and responses. The opinion of the staff was that study packs had encouraged students to cooperate with each other, to test their ideas in discussion and to develop confidence in their own interpretations of texts. Students, they felt, 'did not expect to listen to the teacher all the time but [were more prepared] to talk to each other about their own ideas'. Staff agreed with students that time management and organizational demands had created problems for groups engaged on tasks: some students 'did not use their time properly and panicked at the end'.

Staff were pleased by students' enthusiastic response to the activities:

The presentation went on longer than I had expected because the 'hot seating' of the characters was so successful.

I was pleasantly surprised by the way they took to the work and by their reactions. I think GCSE has prepared them well for this kind of approach.

It can be a useful link between GCSE and A-level, and it makes a refreshing change for upper sixth students too.

One teacher reported on a particularly quiet group of students, generally reluctant to contribute to class discussions. They had become so enthused by the activities in the study pack that lengthy and lively discussion had ensued amongst the whole class and continued beyond the lesson. Another member of staff had been delighted by a video presentation, complete with commentary and background music, produced by one group of students.

Benefits for staff

The production and use of the materials clearly met several of the staff's initially stated requests: staff collaboration increased and teachers valued the chance to work as a team and talk to each other 'about literature and how to teach it'. 'It was good to have time to plan a teaching approach to a text in detail in cooperation with others'. They had welcomed the opportunity 'to look at different teaching styles', especially adopting a facilitative rather than directorial style, and though some did acknowledge a degree of initial unease about using the packs, (e.g., 'I feel a sense of guilt if I'm not standing at the front of the class talking'), all, as already stated, recognized the value of the learning experience for the students. Staff felt the tutorial played a crucial role in helping to keep students on target. Tutorials were also valued by staff for the opportunities they provided to talk to students on an individual basis, suggesting new avenues of research and development for the more able groups, and to give more detailed support to weaker students.

Financial and institutional support

Finally, staff recognized the financial cost of the development. The experience had been worthwhile because time and resources had been made available to the team through the assistance of LEA funding and the cooperation of senior management in the school. This ensured that staff were committed and enthusiastic about Flexible Learning; however, staff also felt its continuation would require further financial input, for the following reasons: the content of the A-level syllabus changes, so that more study packs are needed; also, staff have to have time to meet regularly to maintain the impetus generated so far.

Summary

The introduction of Flexible Learning into the A-level English classroom at Robert Smyth School has undoubtedly been a success for both staff and students. What has been significant has been the degree to which the students have been conscious of discrete skills and taken responsibility for improving them: the parallels between their perceptions and those of the teachers is striking. This is really the crucial point: once students have become aware of the range of skills that they need to develop, and can identify and describe them, they are in a position to be able to work on them. The 'meta-language' of the best Flexible Learning materials does this by reminding students of the need to work to time, to organize themselves into cooperative units, and to plan their presentations. Consequently, as well as developing the relevant skills in the analysis of A-level English Literature, they are setting these skills within a day-to-day working framework of planned tasks, group activities and class presentations. The programme developed at Robert Smyth School, therefore, offers an excellent model for the introduction of the entitlement curriculum.

Subsequent collaborative work with the Robert Smyth English department and other A-level English Literature teachers in Nottinghamshire, Leicestershire, Bedfordshire and Hampshire has produced a substantial amount of material for student-centred work, to be published by Network Educational Press. We here reproduce two exemplars of this (with the kind permission of the publisher): one a Background to Victorian Literature, the other, as an example of text-based work, on *The Great Gatsby*.

THE BACKGROUND TO VICTORIAN LITERATURE

Val Powis, Peter Symonds' College, Winchester

> *This guide will help you to study any text written between 1837-1901. It will help you with examination and coursework preparation.*

Aims

margin notes

This guide will give you the opportunity to:

- Research some of the developments during the Victorian era
- Research eminent Victorian writers
- Identify and explore principal themes and issues in Victorian literature
- Prepare written assignments
- Research other aspects of the Victorian era

Use this box for important information - deadlines, length of your work, assessement, etc

Resources

Many of the books you will need to read will be available in your school's library and in local libraries. Your school's English and History Departments will also possess many helpful texts.

margin notes

The following may be helpful as background material:

- *The Victorian Countryside Vol. 1 & 2.*
  G.E. Mingay

- *The Making of Victorian Literature*
  G. Kitson-Clark

- *Victorian Painters*
  Jeremy Maas

- *Country Life - a Social History of Rural England*
  Howard Newby

- *The Victorian Frame of Mind*
  Walter E. Houghton

Also useful might be:

- **Texts on local history**

- **Other Network Study Guides including:**

    Studying the Long Text at A Level

    Working with Settings

    Victorian Poetry

    Researching a Text

- **Books on art. Artists include:**

Edward Burne Jones	William Dyce	William Morris
George Cruickshank	William Holman Hunt	Dante Gabriel Rossetti
Richard Dadd	Arthur Hughes	
	Ford Madox Brown	

- **Reference Books**

    The Oxford Companion to English Literature

- **Places and Organisations**

    Museums and Art Galleries

    Local Public Record Offices

    Local history organisations

    National Organisations such as:

    English Heritage Education Service (071 973 3441/3)

    The National Trust (071 222 9251)

- **Audio Visual**

    Victorian England P. Clarke Audio Learning
    Available from AVP, Chepstow, 0291 625439

    The Great Exhibition of 1851 Audio Learning
    Available from AVP

    Factories and Their Towns AVP

    How People Lived 1870 - 1970 AVP

margin notes

Activities

Activity 1: The Victorian Period

Use the resources to carry out a short piece of research into the main features of this era. The following topics will help you:

- expansion of towns and cities
- emergence of industrial middle classes
- reading as a leisure activity

Find examples and illustrations for each of the above. Show what each development led to.

If you are studying this period for A Level History draw on your current knowledge.

Use it to make a brief presentation about the Victorian period. Use your research to help you account for this.

Activity 2: Writers of the period

In this activity you will research the prominent writers of the period. Use the resources to do the following:

margin notes

- identify the names of writers to research

- produce a short list of biographical details for each writer

- compile a list of the writer's major works

- identify the themes and subject matter of these major works

Conclude this activity by discussing and listing some of the features which you have found out. For example:

- common themes and concerns in Victorian literature. Are there any variations of subject matter between literary forms?

You might think of other points to list. You might also like to consider why so many writers in this period were women.

Share your responses to these topics with other people in your group.

Draw together what everyone has found out by compiling a wall display on Eminent Victorian Literary Figures.

Activity 3 : An Introduction to Reading Victorian Literature

This activity suggest ways to help you understand the literature of the Victorian Period.

Try to think of Victorian literature as operating on two broad levels.

Level 1 Personal Relationships
Level 2 Public Concerns

The diagram below illustrates these levels. Personal relationships are in the inner circle. Different categories of public concerns are outside it.

Refer to the ideas on the diagram to help you to identify the subject matter of any piece of Victorian literature which you read.

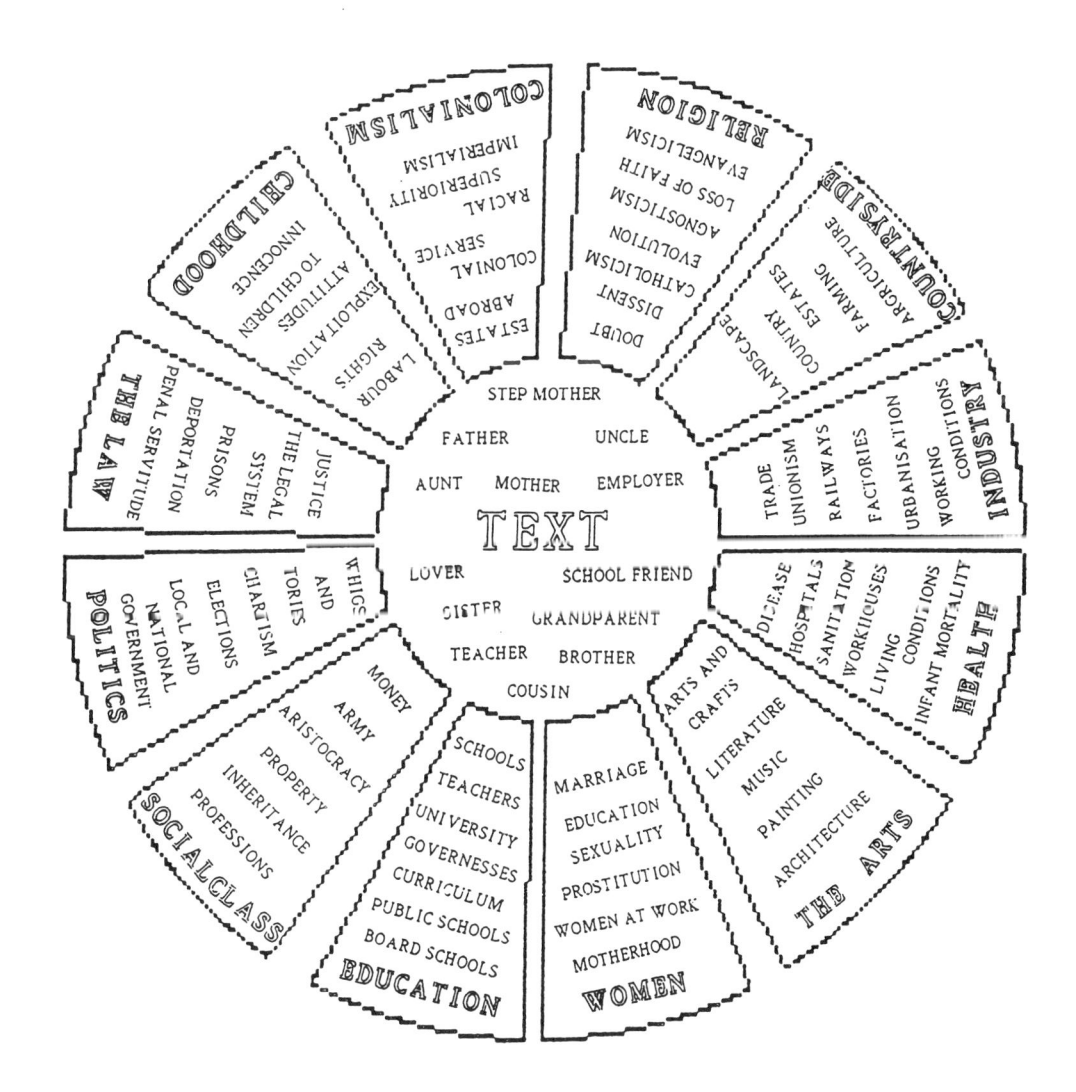

margin notes

Activity 4 : Personal Relationships

This activity shows how you could record the personal relationships dealt with in a text you are reading from Victorian literature.

Always try to do the following:

1) Identify the relationships of the *protagonist* (the main character) which seem to have some bearing on the narrative.

2) Record how these relationships affect the narrative.

You can do this by using a simple table. For example:

Jane Eyre's relationships and their influence on the narrative

Relationship	Influence on the narrative
Jane's orphan status	Establishes the early fortunes of the heroine
Jane's aunt, Mrs Reed	Her dislike for Jane leads to her being sent away to Lowood School
Jane's cousin, St. John Rivers	His offer of marriage provides Jane with an alternative future to the one offered by Rochester
Her uncle in Madeira	Jane's letter to him halts her marriage to Rochester. Her uncle's death gives her financial independence.

margin notes

You can vary the model for recording these relationships.
You could use:

- a separate chart for each relationship
- a key word plan on a large sheet of paper to give you an overview

The Flexible Learning Classroom 65

```
Jane's orphan                              Jane's aunt,
status                                     Mrs Reed
         \                              /
          ┌─────────────────────────┐
          │   Jane's relationships  │
          └─────────────────────────┘
         /                              \
Jane's cousin,                             Jane's uncle
St John Rivers                             in Madeira
```

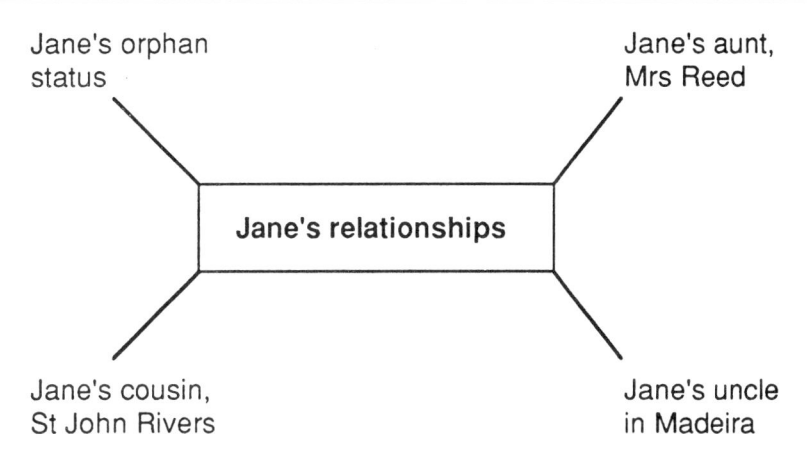

Whichever method you use, keep adding information as you study the texts to ensure you have a clear understanding of the main relationships in the text.

margin notes

Activity 5 : Public Concerns

Use the diagram in Activity Three to remind you of the range of public concerns found in Victorian literature. See what examples you can find in the text you are studying and list them.

For example, in *Jane Eyre*, you will find the subject matter deals with the following issues:

- childhood
- education
- women
- social class
- religion

Keep a detailed record of the way each issue is treated. You could use a chart for each issue:

Issue	Example (Give page/chapter ref) in the narrative	Attitudes expressed by author
Education	• Lowood School • Governess for Adele and the Misses Ingrams	Critical?

You should also spend some time considering why your writer has dealt with these matters of public concern. For example:

- to provide a setting or a context for the narrative?
- to appeal and be relevant to the interests of contemporary audiences?
- to publicise the writer's opinions and influence public opinion?
- to make the plot appear more convincing?

Which other reasons can you think of?

Activity 6 : Linking the Private and Public Worlds

Try to find characters, groups of characters or incidents that bring the two worlds together. Produce a chart that traces each element.

Add any specific authorial comment or background information on your author which indicate his/her major concerns. Identify the public worlds of the Victorian period as they are presented in the text(s) you study.

Extension Activity

margin notes

If you have enjoyed working on Victorian literature you will also find it more interesting and informative to research other Victorian art forms.

1) Use the resources to help you find Victorian paintings and drawings which bear some similarity to the texts you have been reading. Areas of similarity might include

- subject matter
- style (attention to detail, composition)
- moral or social standpoint

2) You could use the same ideas to research photography from this period. Try to find examples of the work of photographers such as Julia Margaret Cameron.

3) You could research the influence of the Victorian period in your own area. Select one of the public concerns you have read about. How did that concern manifest itself in your area during the Victorian period? For example:

Education

- What provision was there in your area before 1837?
- What was the provision by 1901?
- What was the curriculum during this period in local schools?
- Are there Victorian school buildings in your area? How does their design fit in with what you have learned about education from your reading?

You could carry out similar research for any topic which has captured your interest.

THE GREAT GATSBY

Martyn Offord, Bilborough College, Nottingham

> This guide suggests ways to help you understand The Great Gatsby. Through it you will also appreciate one of the main themes in American Literature.

Aims

margin notes

This guide will help you to:

- Research the background to The Great Gatsby
- Examine the novel's narrative technique
- Analyse the characters
- Explore symbolism and structure in the novel

Entitlement at A-level

> *Use this box for important information - deadlines, length of work, assessment, etc.*

Resources

An Introduction to American Literature

- *The Literature of the United States*
  M Cunliffe

Biography

- *Scott Fitzgerald.*
  A Turnbull
- *The Letters of Scott Fitzgerald*
  A Turnbull
- *The Far Side of Paradise;
  A Biography of Scott Fitzgerald*
  Arthur Mizener
- *Zelda Fitzgerald*
  N Milford
- Scott Fitzgerald A Biography
  JS Witley

Literary Criticism

- *F Scott Fitzgerald*
  KGW Cross
- *F Scott Fitzgerald*
  A Mizener

Other works by F. Scott Fitzgerald

- *The Diamond as Big as the Ritz
  and other Stories*
- *The Crack-Up with Other Pieces
  and Stories*
- *The Pat Hibby Stories*
- *Bernice Bobs her Hair and Other
  Stories*
- *The Lost Decade and Other Stories*
- *This Side of Paradise*
- *The Beautiful* and *The Damned*
- *Tender is the Night*
- *The Last Tycoon*

Song Lyrics

- *I Want to be in America* from
  West Side Story
- *Wandering Star* from *Paint
  Your Wagon*

- *The Great Gatsby - A Critical Study*
  Kathleen Pankens
- *The Modern American Novel Chapter 4* Malcolm Bradbury
- *New Essays on The Great Gatsby*
  ed. Matthew Bruccoli
- *The American Novel*
  Andre le Voight
- *FS Fitzgerald - A Collected Criticism*   KE Eble

Film and Video

- *The Great Gatsby.* 1974
- *America.* Alistair Cooke. BBC TV

- *America* from *The Jazz Singer*
  Neil Diamond
- *Follow the Yellowbrick Road* from *The Wizard of Oz*
- *California Dreaming*
  The Mamas and the Papas

Other Network A Level English Guides

- *Narratives and Narrators*
- *Studying Character at A Level*
- *Working with Settings*
- *Researching a Text*
- *Themes at A Level*

You, your group or your teacher may find other resources. List them in this box.

Activities

margin notes | ### Activity 1 : Preliminary Activities

These activities will help you understand the background to *The Great Gatsby*. They focus on:

- Setting
- The American Dream
- The Roaring Twenties

Work in groups to share the research between you.

1) Setting

This activity will give you information about the regions of the United States. You will need this to understand fully the characters in the novel.

Divide a large map of the USA into three vertical bands:

- the East (mark New York and Long Island)
- the Midwest (mark Minnesota)
- the West (mark California, Los Angeles and Hollywood)

'Back East', 'Midwest', 'Out West'. If you know any Americans, ask them what these phrases evoke for them.

2) The American Dream

Explore different dimensions of The American Dream. Look at the following to help you:

- What words are engraved on the Statue of Liberty? What do you think they signify?
- What does the American Constitution say all Americans are entitled to? What view of themselves does this encourage people to hold?
- Which groups of peoples have settled in America during its comparatively short history? What caused them to do this?
- Look at plots of American stories (especially musicals) in which poor people become successful. In what ways are they successful? How can this suggest an American definition of success
- Research the concept of the West as a dream by finding out information about some of the following:
    - migration to California, Oregon Trail, wagon trains, goldrushes
    - the image of California we get from the media, particularly television and films
- Listen to some of the songs listed in the resources. What do lyrics of popular songs tell us about The American Dream?

3) The Roaring Twenties

margin notes

Use the resources to research this period. Produce a collage to show what it was like. Use the following ideas for your images:

- jazz
- fashion
- cars
- parties
- dancers
- gangsters
- films
- bootleggers

You could sandwich your collage between two others. One of the First World War, the other of the Great Depression of the 1930's which followed the Wall Street Crash of 1929. What is the effect of contrasting these eras in this way?

The rest of the activities look at the major elements of the text. Discuss with your teacher which you will do.

Activity 2 : The Narrator

This activity considers the role of Nick Carraway as narrator.

Read the opening four paragraphs of Chapter 1. What explains Nick's role as narrator?

As you read the rest of the novel record what you find out about Nick:

- his background and moral stance
- attitudes towards other characters

Comment on how any of the above might influence the way Nick tells the story.

Continue to keep the role of the narrator clearly in mind as you read the novel. Form opinions about why Fitzgerald told the story through a narrator.

Activity 3 : The Romantic Hero and Heroine

This activity looks at Gatsby and Daisy as romantic hero and heroine.

What is the standard picture of the romantic hero and heroine? Refer to features such as:

- appearance
- background
- feelings for each other

What else can you think of? Use your ideas to assess how well Gatsby and Daisy fit this description.

For example:

	Gatsby: romantic hero	Gatsby: not a romantic hero
Appearance		
Background		
What else?		

Complete a similar chart for Daisy.

Activity 4 : The Characters

It is important that you familiarise yourself with the major characters as you work through the text. Draw columns on sheets of A3 to help you to track what they say and do and what this represents. For example:

Gatsby	Daisy	Jordan	Tom	Myrtle	George Wolfsheim

margin notes

Firstly, for each one record evidence of their:

- enthusiasms
- characteristics
- problems
- attitudes to wealth
- social mannerisms

Explore the significance of the 'dream' for each of the characters from the point of view of:

- reality/illusion
- possible/impossible
- success/failure

- poor/rich
- innocence/corruption
- east/west

When you have finished thenovel write brief descriptions which list the main features of each character, incorporating the elements you have picked out.

margin notes

Activity 5 : Symbolism

This activity explores Fitzgerald's use of symbolism in The Great Gatsby. For example:

Positive symbols

Read carefully Nick's first view of Gatsby. Pick out all the positive symbols such as associations with romance and glamour, such as:

- angels
- green light

Which others can you find?

What picture of Gatsby do we derive from these associations? Record other positive associations as you read through the novel.
Explore also:

- Associations which have both a positive and negative dimension (For example, the yellow car)
- Associations which are entirely negative (ash heaps)
- Associations with the names of female characters (Daisy: white and gold)
- Associations with vision and blindness (Dr Eckleburg)

Explain what each symbol could be associated with and the effect it has on the reader. For example:

Symbols with negative and positive associations

Symbol	Glamorous because	Unpleasant because	Effect on reader
Yellow car			

Associations with women's names

Name	Association	Effect on reader
Daisy	white and gold	

Find and comment on as many examples as you can find for each category.

margin notes

Activity 6 : The Structure of the Novel

This activity suggests a way for you to investigate the novel's structure. As you read the text (or after you have read it:)

- list the events in the order they appear in the book
- list them in their chronological order

What is striking about this structure? What does the writer achieve by it? Refer to the following ideas to support your thinking:

- making connections
- enlisting the reader's sympathy
- understanding the past

Assignment and Presentation Titles

You can write assignments on the following titles or you can use them as a basis for talks and papers to be presented to the rest of your group.

1) 'They were careless people, Tom and Daisy - they smashed up things and creatures and then retreated back into their money or their vast carelessness, or whatever it was that kept them together, and let other people clean up the mess they had made.. Consider each of these accusations against the rich and discuss how *The Great Gatsby* bears these out.

2) Is Gatsby really 'Great'?

3)   To what extent is the novel really about trying to turn back the clock?

4)   How effective is *The Great Gatsby* as a piece of social documentary - that is, giving you an insight into the place and the period in which it is set?

5)   Gatsby is described as 'a platonic conception of himself'. Comment on the appropriateness of this description.

6)   What part does Gatsby's house play in the novel?

7)   Discuss the part played by Nick as the narrator.

8)   Examine the structure of the novel and the way the story is pieced together through flashback and other methods.

Extension Assignments

If you have enjoyed the novel you might like to work on some of the following ideas.

1)   Consider the way the novel has been translated into film. Points to look at include:

- How the film maker dealt with the problem of the narrator
- How verbal images have been translated into visual images
- Where and why new images have been created
- How effectively the structure of the novel has been handled
- How the film has recreated the tone and sympathies of the film

2)   Research Fitzgerald's life and his era. How does an understanding of his life and times enhance an appreciation of the novel?

3) Use video or audio tape to record a tribute to Gatsby. Use interviews, documents and music.

4) Describe some of the events of the book from the points of view of different observers. For example:

- a left wing journalist
- a gossip columnist
- one of the characters in the novel

5) Read other works by Fitzgerald. Contrast characters, plots and themes. Explain any similarities or recurring themes in his work.

References

ALEP (1989) *Aspects of Entitlement*, Occasional Paper No. 1, Leicestershire LEA.
ED (1991) *The Flexible Approach to Learning: A Guide*, Sheffield: Employment Department.
Hardy, P. (1990) Unpublished MA dissertion, University of Leicester.
TA (1989) *TVEI Flexible Learning Project*, Sheffield: Training Agency.
Waterhouse, P. (1983) *Managing the Learning Process*, Maidenhead: McGraw Hill.
Waterhouse, P. (1990) *Flexible Learning: An Outline*, London: Network Educational Press.
Whiteside, T., Sutton, A. and Everton, T. (1992) *16-19 Changes in Education and Training*, London: David Fulton.

CHAPTER 4

Entitlement Areas: Moral Awareness

In the Introduction to this book we made the point that embedding the entitlement curriculum within subject work has two emphases. First, there is the acquisition by the student of skills and competences in styles of learning, cooperation with others and the presentation of their work – processes which have been considered in the first three chapters of this book. Second, and linked to these, is the development of students' personal autonomy and critical awareness: the area of themes and issues. Whilst this is encouraged by the teaching and learning strategies we have been recommending, it needs to be further developed through subject content. In this and the following chapter, we shall show how A-level English Literature can help students to achieve independent perspectives on personal and social issues.

Breadth and balance

In the pre-16 curriculum, concern about the school's role in fostering the growth of 'the whole pupil' has persisted from the inception of the National Curriculum. Lest the proposed core and foundation subjects focused too exclusively upon pupils' academic development, a wide range of cross-curricular themes were recommended to ensure personal and moral growth. To achieve breadth and balance across the whole curriculum for all pupils the National Curriculum Council proposed that the following topics should be included: economic and industrial understanding; education for citizenship; scientific and technological understanding; health education; aesthetic and creative understanding. These topics were to be embedded in the curriculum and taught through the medium of traditional subject matter.

Concern about breadth and balance has featured as prominently in discussions of post-16 provision: hence the emergence of the entitlement curriculum itself. Those planning for the 16–19 cohort have addressed ways of promoting 'the growth of whole student,' and cross-curricular themes have figured as emphatically in their proposals. Their recommendations for cross-curricular themes parallel those of the National Curriculum: science and technology; enterprise and economic awareness; social, political and cultural awareness; values and attitudes; aesthetic awareness; health education. (In early statements of the entitlement curriculum, the categories of 'social/political/cultural awareness' and 'values and attitudes' are the equivalent of the National Curriculum's 'citizenship'; later statements include 'citizenship' explicitly.)

Cross-curricular themes and A-level English Literature

Certain of these thematic areas, particularly social/political/cultural awareness and values and attitudes (citizenship), lend themselves to treatment in the English classroom. We shall show how these can be explored without losing any of the rigour or textual integrity of A-level English Literature. This chapter concentrates on developing students' moral awareness. The following policy statements illustrate the centrality of moral awareness to current ideas about the development of citizenship:

> Moral Codes and Values
>
> Pupils should be helped to develop a personal moral code and explore values and beliefs. Shared values, such as concern for others, industry and effort, self-respect and self-discipline, as well as moral qualities such as honesty and truthfulness, should be promoted and the opportunity be provided for pupils to:
>
> - compare values and beliefs held by themselves and others and identify common ground
> - examine evidence and opinions and form conclusions
> - discuss differences and resolve conflict
> - discuss and consider solutions to moral dilemmas, personal and social
> - appreciate that distinguishing between right and wrong is not always straightforward
> - appreciate that the individual's values, beliefs and moral codes change over time and are influenced by personal experience (e.g. family, friends, media, school, religion and the cultural background in which an individual is raised (NCC, 1990).

This extract from Cambridgeshire LEA's (1989) entitlement document echoes this theme:

> Moral education should aim to provide opportunities to challenge and stimulate students' own moral intuitions in the context of the workplace and in society in general. Topics such as respect for people and concern over their welfare, fairness and justice, truthfulness and integrity and keeping promises and contracts can all be explored to gain understanding of the diversity of beliefs and attitudes. These moral dilemmas can be used in varying contexts e.g. the individual, the firm or organisation, nationally and internationally.

These documents emphasize the belief that autonomous choice should be based on rational decision and discussion, and this view is entirely consistent with the model of entitlement that we have advocated.

Cross-curricular themes: embedding or additionality?

There are two possible strategies for introducing thematic content into the curriculum. First, entitlement issues can be dealt with separately, as some kind of 'additionality'. A number of schools and colleges have taken this path, through core and options programmes, or half-day electives, leaving specialist teachers free to concentrate exclusively on knowledge and appreciation of the set texts. One danger of this approach is that 'additionality' programmes are taken less seriously than mainstream A-level subjects; indeed they may be disregarded completely once the serious business of revision for examination begins. As Peter Mayne puts it: 'the history of attempts to deliver breadth and relevance post-16 as "additionality" is strewn with a litany of failed good intentions' (Mayne, 1990). One might also mention in passing that a school or college whose resources are under strain may find it easier to drop additionality programmes in the interest of saving money.

The second approach is to embed entitlement themes into standard curriculum subjects, and indeed 'the preferred method now is through the enhancement of mainstream studies' (Mayne, 1992). The problem with this approach is that both students and teachers may feel that their subject is being diluted (perhaps even trivialized) and valuable teaching time on syllabus content lost. Even though we shall argue for this method of delivering the thematic content of the entitlement curriculum, these are objections that need to be taken seriously. We do not support any programme that in any way compromises the rigour of A-level analysis, nor the introduction of material into the classroom that takes students away from concentration on their texts. However, as every English teacher knows, classroom discussion of texts has always involved engagement with questions leading outwards into moral, social and cultural issues. We proceed from this recognition, seeing entitlement within the A-level classroom as legitimating precisely those areas of English Literature work. Viewed in this way, the thematic content of entitlement fits without strain into the syllabus: what the concept does is to give a formal structure to discussion that might simply be subsumed under, say, character or theme, rather than emerge in its own right as, say, an issue of moral awareness. More importantly, consciousness of our responsibility to provide entitlement for the whole range of students taking A-level English Literature ought to ensure provision of experiences in the classroom that promote decision-making, cooperation and, above all, a sense of ownership of newly-acquired knowledge. At its heart is a process which takes the student from passive recipient to active learner.

Moral awareness and A-level English Literature

The bearing of literature upon moral development has been a subject for debate ever since Plato argued that fiction was the way to moral confusion and the ruin of the young. Those who have held this view have often gone on to claim that if we restrict the fictional reading of children and young people to morally improving tales, this might encourage them to be 'good'. It is, of course, notoriously difficult to provide evidence for the influence of literature upon morals, either for good or ill. Moreover, any version that looks like the recommendation 'this was a good piece of behaviour – emulate it: this was a bad piece of behaviour – shun it', is suspect on two counts: first, it is not at all clear that such instructions would be followed; and second, even if they were, we should be fostering slavish imitation in our students rather than developing and encouraging their autonomy. Equally suspect is the attempt at an art-morality equation. Any claim that great art (including literature) just *is* morally uplifting is clearly fallacious if we consider the writings of, for example, Beckett and Genet. Rhetorical power and moral goodness do not go hand-in-hand, as every demagogue knows.

In fact, the argument is better pursued in the other direction, by going from ideas about moral development to literature instead of vice versa. The view of moral education proposed by Downey and Kelly (1978): 'to promote in people a desire to achieve the greatest possible knowledge and understanding of whatever kind will help them to reach autonomous choices which are based on careful and informed thinking about the issues involved', has much in keeping with the official policy statements quoted above, and with the notion of entitlement which we are pursuing in this book.

Rather than go from literature to morality on the issue of what constitutes a moral action, it will be more intellectually respectable to start from the philosophical view and then ask whether literature has anything to offer. What, then, are the morally relevant features of any situation? We might distinguish first between the moral and non-moral facts of the case: features like whether or not the object before you is the sort of thing that can have feelings, (thus meriting moral consideration); whether the person before you has blue eyes or brown, is Jewish (none of which detracts from affording full moral consideration), and so on.

Primary here is the notion of respect for persons, the idea that 'the other' must be seen as an end in her or himself, never solely as a means. This view has certain important ramifications for our particular concern with literature. If we recognize that others, with their plans and projects, merit our full attention and consideration, then we have to have some awareness of their feelings, and this involves having some degree of sympathy for them, and empathy with them. The latter involves the notion of 'entering into' their feelings in a fuller way than is implied by the external contemplation of these feelings. And it is here, of course, that the teacher of literature will recognize familiar ground, for it is above all in literature that we see most fully the development of the capacity to enter into the feelings of others.

To sum up the argument so far: moral judgements should be based on autonomous decisions that have considered fully all the morally relevant features of a case: within this the notion of respect for persons is paramount, and full recognition of this involves a degree of empathy with other persons. There is wide support for the place of literature in aiding this business of 'entering into' the feelings of others:

> It [literature] provides imaginative insight into what another person is feeling; it allows the contemplation of possible human experiences which the

reader has not met. . . . It confronts the reader with problems similar to his own, and does it at the safety of one remove (Bullock Report 1, 1975, ch. 9).

And, from a NATE document (1976):

> More profitable in the long term than direct confrontation with the most obvious relevant issues is the constant discussion of situations in novels which deal with the way people treat each other, how scapegoats are created, outsiders persecuted, those who move into new environments have problems, those who relate to each other across different sections of society are persecuted, etc. Since these situations recur again and again in poems, stories and novels, the teacher is creating a sense of unity of human experience. . . .

In the five passages for classroom use which follow, we show how these points can be exemplified within the traditional pattern of literary analysis.

1. Considering respect for persons as persons

Passage 1

> *Shylock*: He hath disgraced me and hindered me half a million, laughed at my losses, mocked at my gains, scorned my nation, thwarted my bargains, cooled my friends, heated mine enemies, and what's his reason? I am a Jew. Hath not a Jew eyes? Hath not a Jew hands, organs, dimensions, senses, affections, passions? Fed with the same food, hurt with the same weapons, subject to the same diseases, healed by the same means, warmed and cooled by the same winter and summer as a Christian is? If you prick us, do we not bleed? If you tickle us, do we not laugh? If you poison us, do we not die?
>
> (*Merchant of Venice*, Act 3, sc.(i) 49–60)

In groups of 4 or 5, answer the following questions

1. What has happened to Shylock?
2. What reason does Antonio have for doing this?
3. What objections does Shylock make to this as a justification? What do you feel about these objections?

Whole class: on the basis of group answers, discuss the idea of morally relevant/irrelevant facts in the treatment of persons.

Passage 2

Another passage where students are invited to consider the issue of respect for persons is the episode of the pandybat in the first section of James Joyce's *Portrait of the Artist as a Young Man* (Penguin, 1974, pp. 50–51). Here the more extended nature of the passage allows a fuller investigation of the ways that respect for persons and the relevant facts of the case bear upon the treatment of Stephen, and thus upon the nature of justice. The questions for students are followed by an explanatory passage showing how the various moral steps can be explicated.

1. What are your feelings about Stephen from the information you get on pp50-51?
2. What is the situation over his glasses, and how does Father Arnall respond to it?
3. What is the difference between Fleming and Stephen?
4. How is Stephen treated by Father Dolan, the prefect of studies?
5. On what grounds is he treated thus?
6. In what ways is Father Dolan respecting/not respecting Stephen as a person?
7. Do you agree that the treatment was 'cruel and unfair'? Give your reasons.
8. Taking account of Father Arnall's treatment of Stephen and of Fleming, what comment do you want to make about him?

In the passage, the reader's respect for Stephen as a person comes from the information Joyce gives us about all the characters involved in the incident. Stephen is conscientious, obedient and honest; we know from his achievements in class that he is clever, and from Father Arnall that he has genuinely broken his glasses. We know too that he is different from the other pupil involved, Fleming, who was being punished for writing a bad Latin theme. Crucially, we know that Father Arnall exempted Stephen from writing because he believed him. The prefect of studies, however, condemns him as a 'lazy little schemer' because that is how Father Dolan views all pupils who are not obviously working: in other words, he has no respect for persons as persons, and is not prepared to listen to any of the relevant facts of the case. As with Shylock, so with Stephen: he is punished, despite the extenuating circumstances, simply because he is a boy, and 'boys' and 'tricks' are synonymous. We assent wholeheartedly with Stephen when he thinks 'it was cruel and unfair . . . it was unfair and cruel' – a moral judgement upon the prefect of studies which seems quite appropriate: he is no respecter of persons, he is not prepared to listen to relevant facts of the case.

What comes across most strongly in this passage is the rhetorical power with which Joyce conveys Stephen's sense of injustice as well as pain. There is constant repetition of the key words that shape the moral situation ('cruel', 'unfair', 'trick', 'schemer'). Moreover, close observation shows how badly the adults come out of the situation of total power which they abuse: Father Dolan clearly derives sadistic pleasure from his beatings of the boys, while Father Arnall, who is more sympathetic, seems devoid of any powers of judgement. In treating Fleming (who had done badly) and Stephen (who was unfairly punished) in the same way at the end of the episode, he makes no discrimination between the two, thus giving Stephen yet another legitimate reason for feeling unjustly treated. As powerfully conveyed in this passage as Stephen's feelings of injustice are his feelings of pain, and the reader, empathizing with the feeling of injustice which the boy experiences, is drawn also into the acuteness of the pain. Nonetheless, in this case his feelings and the justice of the situation are two separate issues: he isn't unjustly treated because he feels unjustly treated; he isn't unjustly treated because he feels pain (a genuinely transgressing boy would after all feel the same pain). In short, Stephen's feelings are consequent upon the unjust situation, not something that makes the situation unjust.

2. Considering respect for persons as persons, and beginning to look at the role of feelings

The role of feelings, however, is not always in a consequentialist position; it can be, and indeed often is, part of the moral situation itself. This is clearly seen in the next passage where Lear's (and by extensions anyone's) feelings about how he personally is being treated in the situation is part of our condemnation of Goneril and Regan.

Passage 3

Goneril: Hear me, my Lord
What need you five-and-twenty, ten, or five,
To follow in a house, where twice so many
Have a command to tend you?

Regan: What need one?

Lear: O! reason not the need; our basest beggars
Are in the poorest thing superfluous:
Allow not nature more than nature needs,
Man's life is cheap as beast's. Thou art a lady:
If only to go warm were gorgeous,
Why, nature needs not what thou gorgeous wear'st,
Which scarcely keeps thee warm. But for true need –
You heavens, give me that patience, patience I need!
You see me here, you gods, a poor old man,
As full of grief as age; wretched in both
If it be you that stirs these daughters' hearts
Against their father, fool me not so much
To bear it tamely; touch me with noble anger,
And let not women's weapons, water-drops,
Stain my man's cheeks! No, you unnatural ways,
I will have such revenges on you both
That all the world shall – I will do such things
What they are, yet I know not – but they shall be
The terrors of the earth. You think I'll weep;
No, I'll not weep:
I shall have full cause of weeping, but this heart
Shall break into a hundred thousand flaws
Or ere I'll weep. O Fool! I shall go mad.
(*King Lear*, Act 2 sc.(iv) 259–85)

In groups of 4 or 5, answer these questions:

1. What is Goneril's and Regan's reason for saying that Lear doesn't need any private servants of his own?

2. If reason is to be used as the sole criterion, says Lear, what would people need?
3. What would life then be like?
4. Do Lear's daughters live up to this reasoning in the conduct of their own lives?
5. Summarize Lear's feelings in this speech. To what extent do you sympathize with him?

Whole class: through discussion of answers 1–5, students should start to explore the issue of feelings as a relevant factor in the consideration of moral issues.

In each of these exercises, a further dimension can be introduced by having the group appoint an observer. The observer's task is to note:

(i) how the group handles disagreement
(ii) if everyone who wants to speak is given an opportunity
(iii) if consensus is reached, and if not, how the minority view is heard
(iv) if points are argued for, or just stated.

After each activity the observer should report back to the group. At the end of the series the group should reflect on whether each member of the group was treated with respect and sensitivity, whether anyone was, or felt, left out. In other words, was respect for persons reflected in the behaviour of the group members towards each other?

3. The role of feelings, and feelings and judgement

Passage 4: Judgement from outside the text

The teacher keen to allow students to explore the structure of moral argument will have to go further than this, for literature does not always keep the balance between judgement and empathy. When this balance is lost, the reader's sympathy for a certain character can elide appropriate moral distinctions, and if we are to incorporate the dimension of moral awareness successfully into students' reading, we have to find ways to enable students to see that such imbalance can be redressed. There is still a world beyond that of the text, and from that world appropriate moral distinctions can be brought to bear on the text. Fortunately an aspect of the reading process itself can be drawn on here.

The words of the Bullock Report (1975) ('[A]t the safety of one remove') reminded us that the reader is both within the events of the text and outside them. The reader comes under the sway of various sets of feelings while reading the text, sympathizing with one character and condemning another. However, because she or he is also outside the text ('at the safety of one remove'), a more ample perspective upon it is also possible, a perspective which can include wider considerations, like justice and fairness.

This perspective can be teased out through class discussion, as the following example illustrates. The short story 'Uncle Earnest' from Alan Sillitoe's *The Loneliness of the Long-Distance Runner* was worked on by a group in the transition phase from GCSE to A-level. The instruction given was very open: 'As you read this story, write down any feelings you have about the main character, any other characters and the outcome of the story'. Here are some of the student responses:

> The end of the story made me feel depressed and I felt like crying. I pitied him. The people in the cafe were wrong to report him, they knew he meant no harm. I thought it was wrong of the police threatening him, because he had no criminal background. I am sure if he dressed neat he wouldn't have been questioned (Sylvia).
>
> Lonely man, sad meaningless life, needed friendship. Policemen showed no compassion or understanding. They were outsiders looking in, presuming without knowing the full facts or circumstances. The natural reaction is to feel sorry for the man, because we know the inside story (Carol).
>
> My first impression was to feel he's the kind of person I would try to avoid talking to, because he is dirty-looking and sounds like a tramp. He sounds very lonely as he lives in a boarding house and no one seems to care for him. He is very quiet and timid. But he is a loving man, who wants to help and care for people. It was wrong to take away his happiness. . . . I feel very sorry for him because everyone is judging him by his appearance and noone (especially the police) gave him the chance to speak for himself (Maggie).
>
> A deeply lonely man. . . . Feel sorry for him. . . . Society cannot take anything that is different. Ready to jump to conclusions, want to protect the children, no one else knows the circumstances. . . . Feel very sad for him, pity him. Because he isn't looked upon as respectable by society, back to the depths of loneliness. Why can't people mind their own business? Police unsympathetic. I have an understanding for the poor man, many people like that about. . . . Feel contempt for people's morals. They know nothing, understand little and are so narrow-minded (Maureen).
>
> The main feeling I get is one of pity and sorrow for Uncle Earnest. It was so unfair the way he was misunderstood. I feel sorry for the two policemen . . . they twisted the story into something smutty and perverted. Due to years in the police force their minds have been affected so they see sex and violence as everyday things and have forgotten human qualities such as kindness and friendship. Kindness is regarded with immediate suspicion by them (Annabel).

Only one girl stepped outside the pull of Sillitoe's rhetoric, for Carol went on to say:

> But the chances are, if I saw the same thing happening in a cafe in town, I would be very suspicious, and would not show the same kind of sympathy, because I wouldn't know the inside story. It's important, though, maybe I'd try to find out more before I jump to conclusions.

Clearly, in this example there has been whole-hearted 'entering into' the feelings of Uncle Earnest, and the wider perspective ('Well, what if . . .? How could you be sure?') is one that, in this case, was reached independently by only one of the students. The wider perspective was in fact teased out in class through further work, in small group settings and role play.

Passage 5: Judgement from inside the text

A text where the perspective is differently managed is the Katherine Mansfield short story *The Young Girl*. In this story the central character behaves badly throughout. She speaks 'wearily' to her mother, gives orders sharply to her young brother and 'carelessly' to the hotel waitresses. She behaves ungraciously to the narrator, displays boredom, contempt and impatience during tea, a character unlikely at first to elicit much sympathy from the reader.

Is there, however, another perspective worth seeking? Might there be an explanation within the text which, if not arousing sympathy, encourages suspension of premature judgement upon unpleasant behaviour? Why might she behave like this? What are the facts of the case . . .? She has travelled widely in great luxury and has been prematurely exposed to sophisticated settings. That is the broad context. The immediate context demands closer examination, created as it is by the young girl's mother: the casino; the clamorous friend; the carelessness with money. Mrs Raddick and Mrs McEwan quickly forget the children after dispatching them to tea and are, of course, nowhere to be seen on their return.

Whilst none of this makes the young girl likeable, it goes far toward explaining her affected, dismissive behaviour in public places. We like Hennie far more but, when we reflect upon his sister's response to being left to wait for their mother, we realize that Katherine Mansfield intends that we shift away from the judgement encouraged by most of the story. Her arrogance and rudeness have been displaced by hesitation and powerful emotion, 'I'm always waiting – in all kinds of places . . .'. Her earlier behaviour, in retrospect, may have been untrue to an inner-self which, we are given the evidence to suggest, had to be protected against the insensitivity of other people.

What happens as this very short story proceeds is that our perspective on 'the young girl' (she is never named) lengthens – at first we were closely confronted by her rudeness which struck us sharply by its brusqueness. Later, however, we began to assimilate details of the background around her: everyone except her brother is older, she is handed round like a parcel, stared at by older men like an object. Moving in a milieu where the 'sophisticated' response to everything is to sneer at it, she adopts this style of speech partly to be 'grown up', partly as a protective covering. Yet she keeps slipping back in to the greedy behaviour of a child being given treats (the chocolate, the cakes, the ice-cream), while despising and being mortified by the greed as well as the behaviour of the 12-year-old brother. We come to see how marooned she is between childhood and adulthood and come to share the perspective of the narrator, who watches and waits carefully throughout the story, seeming to sense that something more is going on and content to wait for it to emerge. The narrator and the reader, if they have attended to the complex pattern of feeling beneath the words and behaviour of the girl, are 'rewarded' at the end. When she realizes that her mother isn't waiting for her, the sophisticated mask dissolves: she is once more the abandoned child, and is, moreover, anxious that others shouldn't be put out in any way, or allowed to see her disappointment . . . 'I – I didn't mind it a bit', etc. Even the speech patterns have broken down here.

It isn't that we come to like the young girl at the end of the story so much as that we come to see we know nothing about her at all except that she is stranded between two generations, afraid, insecure and self-protective. That doesn't mean that she's nice, but it does mean that all the language upon which we had based our earlier view of her has to be seen in a new light – we have entered into her feelings, but through the eyes of the narrator, with a distance and separate perspective. We have come to sympathize with her dilemma.

Here, then, feelings and judgement are held within the framework of the story in the way well described by Robert Heilman (1973):

> ... literature of quality ministers to sympathy and understanding without making them too easy and without getting too sloppy about it. It engages our sympathy, but keeps the object of sympathy in full perspective. It elicits at once warmth of feeling and coolness of judgement. It does not merely set us afloat on a wash of feeling, which is the way of sentimentality, or set us up high and dry on the judgement seat of principle, which is the way of lecture and homily. It draws us in but holds us out; even when we are emphatically engaged, we remain contemplative onlookers (p. 24).

It is important that we clarify precisely what claim we have been making in this chapter. The moral argument emphasizes agent autonomy, the importance of distinguishing the morally relevant facts of the case, and the role of feelings in moral decision. The structure of this argument is not dependent in any way on theories of literature or discussion of literary form. Thus, we are not claiming that good literature makes you good (or that bad literature makes you bad). Our claim is simply that literature can offer powerfully-expressed examples of the range of considerations relevant to moral judgement and thinking, and that these considerations can be worked through by students through the familiar practices of literary analysis of texts. In this way, engaging with the literary content of the passage is of a piece with engagement with the moral issues and arguments. Any further question of influence on the structure of students' own moral thinking is not an argument about literature as such, but only one about general human response to morally relevant language of any sort. Literature can show ways of making a total moral response to a situation: the fact that we do not all go and behave thus demonstrates our ability to switch moral responses on and off. It is characteristic of literature that it keeps pushing moral considerations back at the reader: it is the prerogative of the reader to ignore these promptings.

Moral awareness and A-level English Literature: whole-text approaches

Thus far in this chapter, we have shown how a range of texts and extracts can, through processes quite familiar to the A-level literature classroom, be analysed to give a morally developmental progression. Such an approach can be quite attractive for a number of reasons: if points of some moral complexity need to be elucidated for full (literary) understanding of a text, the passages above, or similar ones, could be used to work through the relevant moral points. However, patterns of increasing moral complexity can emerge in and through a single text, which might offer sufficient richness and scope for the drawing of similar patterns of moral discrimination. The following two examples, both dealing with books familiar to A-level syllabuses, illustrate this. Common to both approaches are teaching strategies that encourage students to be responsible for their judgements when confronted with moral situations in a text.

The Heart of the Matter

Any treatment of this text in the A-level classroom will involve discussion of the moral and spiritual distinctions Greene draws. The moral dimension invites the reader to make judgements of increasing complexity as she or he reads: judgements that must be based upon awareness of and response to the language of the novel. Take, for example, the Syrian storekeeper, Yusuf. The student has to see that the apparently contradictory description of Yusuf's face as 'wide, pasty, untrustworthy, sincere', is in fact an accurate description of the complexity of his relation to the central character, Scobie, as this emerges in the course of the book. There is moral complexity, too, in the depiction of Wilson. Greene's treatment of both of these characters is part of the book's larger concern with concepts of justice, compassion and responsibility as they bear on what Greene sees as the complexity of human nature, and the reader is invited to consider these in considerable detail during study of the book. These observations are part of any A-level teaching programme of the novel. They also form part of the provision of the moral awareness dimension of the entitlement curriculum. Students can be asked to think through Greene's argument for themselves if they are presented with an appropriate selection of material for discussion and examination. Consider the following excerpts (Penguin, 1972):

> Round the corner, in front of the old cotton tree, where the earliest settlers has gathered their first day on the unfriendly shore, stood the law courts and police station, a great stone building like the grandiloquent boast of weak men. Inside that massive frame the human being rattled in the corridors like a dry kernel. No one could have been adequate to so rhetorical a conception. But the idea in any case was only one room deep. In the dark narrow passage behind, in the charge-room and the cells, Scobie could always detect the odour of human meanness and injustice – it was the smell of a zoo, of sawdust, excrement, ammonia, and lack of liberty. The place was scrubbed daily, but you could never eliminate the smell (p. 15).
>
> he soon discovered that the guilt and innocence were as relative as the wealth (p. 20).
>
> Why do I love this place so much? Is it because here human nature hasn't had time to disguise itself? Nobody here could ever talk about a heaven on earth. Heaven remained rigidly in its proper place on the other side of death, and on this side flourished the injustices, the cruelties, the meanness that elsewhere people so cleverly hushed up. Here you could love human beings nearly as God loved them, knowing the worst: you didn't love a pose, a pretty dress, a sentiment artfully assumed (p. 36).
>
> . . . the church was empty. Scobie sat down at the back: he had no inclination to pray – what was the good? If one was a Catholic, one had all

the answers: no prayer was effective in a state of mortal sin, but he watched the other two with sad envy. They were still inhabitants of the country he had left. This was what human love had done to him – it had robbed him of love for eternity. . . .

He said, O God, I am the only guilty one because I've known the answers all the time. I've preferred to give you pain rather than give pain to Helen or my wife because I can't observe your suffering. I can only imagine it. But there are limits to what I can do to you – or them. I can't desert either of them while I'm alive, but I can die and remove myself from their blood stream. They are ill with me and I can cure them. And you too, God, – you are ill with me. I can't go on, month after month, insulting you. . . . You'll be better off if you lose me once and for all. I know what I'm doing. I'm not pleading for mercy. I am going to damn myself, whatever that means. I've longed for peace and I'm never going to know peace again. But you'll be at peace when I am out of your reach. . . . You'll be able to forget me, God, for eternity (pp. 257–8).

'He was a bad Catholic.'
'That's the silliest phrase in common use,' Father Rank said.
'And at the end this – horror. He must have known that he was damning himself.'
'Yes, he knew that all right. He never had any trust in mercy – except for other people.'
'It's no good even praying . . .'
Father Rank clapped the cover of the diary to and said furiously, 'For goodness sake, Mrs Scobie, don't imagine you – or I – know a thing about God's mercy.' (pp. 271–2).

On the basis of extracts like these, students can be asked what they think Greene is saying about justice, judgement and mercy. They will be considering these in a number of contexts that include the British/colonial dimension, Scobie's responses to a variety of situations, and the author's comments about how much we can know of God's judgement and mercy. Students' ideas about these moral issues will be developing out of the concepts we outlined earlier: respect for persons, feelings, judgement and compassion. The text itself confront the students with these moral concepts.

Pride and Prejudice

Distinctions are drawn by Jane Austen throughout *Pride and Prejudice* between characters' ability to judge each other accurately and to make what in her view is the appropriate moral response to situations. This ability is explained partly by their possession of accurate information but mainly by individual moral worth. Students might analyse and discuss in detail the episode of Lydia Bennet's and George Wickham's elopement. This offers them an opportunity to identify a novelist's view of characters' differing judgements and responses to a situation. It also invites them to make decisions about characters' relative dependence upon accurate information and about the individual moral worth of each.

Chapter 51 describes the couple's arrival and short stay at Longbourne after their elopement and marriage. It involves, therefore, the whole of the Bennet family, each of whom anticipates their arrival and responds to it in different ways. Close examination of this chapter might be the culmination of a series of investigations into different members of the Bennet family's state of knowledge about Wickham, that is, how strong a position each of them is in to assess his seduction of Lydia at Brighton, and into their capacity for appropriate moral response to his behaviour. Along the way, two interesting questions might be explored: how likely is it that Lydia would have behaved better has she known what Darcy and Elizabeth had concealed about Wickham's attempted seduction of Georgiana? How likely is it that Mrs Bennet's presence in Brighton would, as she claims, have prevented the elopement?

It might be useful, first, for students to find out who knows how much about Wickham. For whilst only Jane and Elizabeth know about his ignominious behaviour in Derbyshire to Darcy and to his sister, and the accompanying calumny about the Darcy family, his sudden mercenary attachment to Miss King and her family's removal of her into safety is widely known. If we take Lydia as the central figure in this episode, we find that not only does she know about his shifting affection but, as Elizabeth observes, she must be aware of the sudden nature of his passion for her, given 'there was no (earlier) symptom of passion on either side'.

Clearly it is understandable that Elizabeth and Jane are most troubled about the elopement because they, as a result of Darcy's letter, know about Wickham's perfidious behaviour in the past. That, however, is only part of the explanation of their withdrawal of sympathy from the couple and their astonishment at their insouciant behaviour in Chapter 51. What must be examined are those distinctions which derive from differences in powers of observation, sensitivity to the effects of one's behaviour upon others and apppropriateness of responses to occasion. At one end of Jane Austen's moral spectrum are Lydia and her mother. Students might be asked to trace their behaviour from the beginning of this episode – the visit to Brighton – until its conclusion. Between them and Elizabeth, who returns to the refuge of her room 'sick of this folly', and Kitty and Mary, shallow in their different ways, are Mr Bennet whose 'chief wish . . . was to have as little trouble in the business as possible' and the generous-minded Jane.

The point of this exploration is to strengthen students' sense of the distinctions a novelist draws between his or her characters' responses to events and to notice upon what these are based. Mrs Bennet and Lydia are treated very harshly by Jane Austen. Given the extent of their insensitivity to the feelings of others, is this justified? Mr Bennet too, in his apathy and bitterness, is similarly harshly judged. Again, on the evidence of his behaviour to his wife and daughters, to what extent is this justified? Wherein lie the differences between Jane's and Elizabeth's shame and embarrassment over the Lydia/Wickham marriage and the merriment and ostentation of their mother and youngest sister?

Encouraging moral awareness through literature in the ways we have discussed above can alert students to the complexity of individual moral situations. Students, given opportunities to develop a mature and rational perspective, may thus avoid making superficial generalizations in the moral decisions of real life. George Eliot puts the case persuasively in *The Mill on the Floss*:

> . . . moral judgements must remain false and hollow unless they are

checked and enlightened by a perpetual reference to the special circumstances that mark the individual lot.

All people of broad, strong sense have an instinctive repugnance for the men of maxims because such people early discern that the mysterious complexity of our life is not to be embraced by maxims and that to lace ourselves up in formulas of that sort is to repress all the divine promptings and inspirations that spring from growing insight and sympathy. And the man of maxims is the popular representative of the minds that are guided in their moral judgement solely by general rules, thinking that these will lead them to justice by a ready-made patent method, without the trouble of exerting patience, discrimination, impartiality, without any care to assure themselves whether they have the insight that comes from a hardly-earned estimate of temptation or from a life vivid and intense enough to have created a wide, fellow feeling with all that is human. (Signet edition, pp. 520-21.)

References

Bullock, Sir A. (1975) *A Language for Life*, London: HMSO.
Cambridgeshire LEA (1989) Entitlement document, author.
Downey, M. and Kelley, A. V. (1978) *Moral Education: Theory and Practice*, London: Harper and Row.
Heilman, R. (1973) *The Ghost on the Ramparts*, Athens, GA: University of Georgia Press.
Mayne, P. (1990) *Effective Learning – Pedagogy in the A Level Classroom: Into a New ERA*, London: David Fulton.
Mayne, P. (1992) in Whiteside, T. *et al.* (eds) *16-19 Changes in Education and Training*, London: David Fulton.
NATE (1976) *The Teaching of English in Multicultural Britain*, Sheffield: NATE.
NCC (1990) *Education for Citizenship, Curriculum Guidance No. 8*, York: NCC.

CHAPTER 5

Economic Awareness, Political and Social Issues

We turn now to two other themes of the entitlement curriculum where the special features of literature have a distinct place: those of economic awareness and of political and social issues. Our argument here has something in common with our argument in the previous chapter, particularly in its emphasis on the notion of empathy. Literature offers ampleness of scope. It goes beyond the mere description of particular economic or political arrangements into the writer's examination of the interpenetration of the personal and the social in the lives of the characters in the text. We shall point to examples in texts where one can see at work writers' ideas of how people shape and are shaped by what they do, and the political and economic circumstances under which they do it. We argue that this kind of examination gives the student the perspective necessary for maturity in both personal and social life. We want our students to look beyond the superficial appearances of things and to question why they are so: we want also to nurture in them the wish to work out for themselves the things they value.

This breadth of perspective can emerge naturally and without strain from the traditional work of the A-level English classroom: the only change is that, in giving social and political issues a formal structure and foregrounding when they are present in a text, we are pointing up their separateness as issues from the text, and inviting students themselves to learn to make these distinctions. As with books, so with life: it does not come at you transparently, offering you the only way of seeing things, though such is the density of everyday life that it seems so and, of course, we spend much of our childhood believing that it is so. If students can come to see how, in books, people and environments shape each other, then they will perhaps have more insight into how this is so in their own lives. They may indeed be more empowered to act in that environment (and Part 2 of this book will demonstrate how this can emerge from the Communication Studies work). However, we argue that the special feature of literature is to go beyond mere contemplation of the world as it is: insofar as it offers versions of the world or of social arrangements different from our own, it pushes questions at us: Why is this so? What happens when people live like this? Since we inevitably use our own experiences as points of departure when considering other versions, literature encourages further questions: How do we live? Why is this so? Students engaged in this kind of questioning have the opportunity not just to become effective agents within the established structures of their own society, but to develop views on why that society is as it is.

As with the issue of moral awareness in the previous chapter, support for these aims comes both from National Curriculum and from entitlement statements. The National Curriculum Guidance on Citizenship (NCC, 1990, pp. 3-4) has this to say:

KNOWLEDGE
Pupils should develop knowledge and understanding of the following:

the nature of community
- the variety of communities to which people simultaneously belong: family, school, local, national, European and worldwide
- how communities combine stability with change
- how communities are organised and the importance of rules and laws
- how communities reconcile the needs of individuals with those of society

roles and relationships in a democratic society
- the nature of co-operation and competition between individuals, groups and communities
- similarities and difference between individuals, groups and communities – diversity and interdependence
- the experience and opportunities of people in different roles and communities

and, on **ATTITUDES**
- independence of thought on social and moral issues
- respect for different ways of life, beliefs, opinions and ideas
- respect for rational argument and non-violent ways of resolving conflict
- active concern for human rights
- appreciate that the individual's values, beliefs and moral codes change over time and are influenced by personal experience (e.g. of the family, friends, the media, school, religion and cultural background in which an individual is raised.)

It is surprising that National Curriculum statements about 'Citizenship' make so little use of the resources of literature in activities for promoting citizenship. It suggests only that children be read stories at Key Stage 1 (*The Tiger who Came to Tea*, *The Three Little Pigs*). Any teacher of literature, reading the above recommendations, will readily see how literature provides rich resources for this work.

While many entitlement statements for the 16-19 cohort mention Economic and Political awareness, there is little specific guidance on appropriate teaching material. The Cambridgeshire statement says:

Students should develop their abilities to make rational judgements about the community in which they live and understand the relationship of that community to others both nationally and internationally.

Many post-16 programmes of study contribute to progression in this area by providing a range of contexts in which students can acquire knowledge and develop skills. Students need to understand basic economic ideas such as the scarcity of resources, wealth creation and distribution, if they are to participate positively as a (sic) producer, consumer and citizen able to evaluate the economic aspects of decision making. Students need to consider how economic decision making can affect individuals, families, firms and the local, national and international community.

Group activities in this area of entitlement can be particularly effective. Involving students in considering the needs and viewpoints of other group members demonstrates the problematic nature of decision making. Moral, political, environmental and equal opportunities themes can be integrated with economic and industrial awareness, so that students' decision making is informed by appropriate knowledge, concepts and skills (Cambridgeshire LEA, 1989).

Any introduction of these topics into the A-level English classroom must of course observe the same conditions that we enjoined upon ourselves in Chapter 4. This work must not take the students away from the proper study of their texts, and the activities we propose should not conflict with the general teaching programme. Nonetheless, though it will not be true of all texts, and even when it is, it will be true to a greater or lesser degree, there is much that can be done entirely within the parameters of the normal A-level teaching schedule.

Take for example, Scott Fitzgerald's *Tender is the Night*. A key factor in the moral decay of Dick Diver is the gradually destructive influence on him of the Warren money for, though he tries to keep himself separate from it, its exponential increase, and the task of managing it, absorbs more and more of the Divers' time ('there was now so much money that the mere spending of it, the care of goods, was an absorption in itself'). Worse, it seems by its very lavishness to trivialize anything he might achieve in his psychological work. However, the theme of economic influence is not limited to the treatment of Dick. Consider the following passage:

With Nicole's help Rosemary bought two dresses and two hats and four pairs of shoes with her money. Nicole bought from a great list that ran to two pages, and bought the things in the windows besides. Everything she liked that she couldn't possibly use herself, she bought as a present for a friend. She bought coloured beads, folding beach cushions, artificial flowers, honey, a guest bed, bags, scarfs, love birds, miniatures for a doll's house, and three yards of some new cloth the colour of prawns. She bought a dozen bathing suits, a rubber alligator, a travelling chess set of gold and ivory, big linen handkerchiefs for Abe, two chamois leather jackets of kingfisher blue and burning bush from Hermes – bought all these things not a bit like a high-class courtesan buying underwear and jewels, which were after all professional equipment and insurance, but with an entirely different point of view. Nicole was the product of much ingenuity and toil. For her sake trains began their run at Chicago and traversed the round belly of the continent to California; chicle factories fumed and link belts grew link by link in factories; men mixed toothpaste in vats and drew mouthwash out of copper hogsheads; girls canned tomatoes quickly in August or worked rudely at the Five-and-Tens on Christmas Eve; half-breed Indians toiled on Brazilian coffee plantations and dreamers were muscled out of patent rights in new tractors – these were some of the people who gave a tithe to Nicole and, as the whole system swayed and thundered onward, it lent a feverish bloom to such processes of hers as wholesale buying, like the flush on a fireman's face holding his post before a spreading blaze. She illustrated very simple principles, containing in herself her own doom, but illustrated them so accurately that there was grace in the procedure, and presently Rosemary would try to imitate it. (Penguin, 1986, p. 65).

Apart from the passing, and unelaborated, reference to a Marxist perspective, this passage illustrates Fitzgerald's view not only of the interpenetration of parts of society with each other, but the ways in which individuals are shaped by them. This is clear in the case of the 'operatives' who service the great machine of conspicuous consumption and depend on it for employment, but Fitzgerald's passage also brings out the extent to which Nicole, absurdly rich and apparently free, is equally enmeshed in the machine, though of course she is far better able to handle its effects than Dick, since she accepts her role as conspicuous consumer, having been bred to it. Taken with Fitzgerald's reflections on the differences between the North and the South, and the frenzied social activity of the Jazz Age, these points add up to a view of characters and their relationships that blends the influence of social, cultural and economic environment with the temperamental and psychological differences between persons.

Such features are going to be part of the teaching programme of the novel but, highlighted in the way we have done, they allow students to see more clearly how writers suggest that such factors influence lives. Indeed, to refer briefly back to the previous chapter, part of our judgement of characters will depend on how we view this question of influence.

Attitudes to change

Part of the ampleness of vision that literature offers lies in the range of attitudes displayed and the possibilities this offers students for a measured weighing up of a number of perspectives. Students are thus given scope for critical questioning both of the views that are put forward in texts and views they may hold themselves. This is illustrated by the following exercise, which asks students to consider different attitudes taken by writers to the question of change.

The first of these extracts comes from *The Rainbow* (D.H. Lawrence, 1915) and the second from *The First Futurist Manifesto* (1909). Students, after being given brief introductions to the passages and hearing them aloud, can be asked to discuss, in groups of four or five, the questions that follow:

'But is this place as awful as it looks?' the young girl asked, a strain in her eyes.
'It is just what it looks,' he said. 'It hides nothing.'
A long discussion of the place and the people followed between them.
  Ursula sat black-souled and very bitter, hearing the two of them talk. There seemed something ghoulish even in their very deploring of the state of things. They seemed to take a ghoulish satisfaction in it.
  The pit was the great mistress. Ursula looked out of the window, and saw the proud, demon-like colliery with her wheels twinkling in the heavens,

the formless, squalid mass of the town lying aside. It was the squalid heap of side-shows. The pit was the main show, the raison d'etre of it all.

How terrible it was! There was a horrible fascination in it – human bodies and lives subjected in slavery to that symmetric monster of the colliery. There was a swooning, perverse satisfaction in it. For a moment she was dizzy.

Then she recovered, felt herself in a great loneliness, wherein she was sad but free. She had departed. No more would she subscribe to the great colliery, to the great machine which has taken us all captives. In her soul, she was against it, she disowned even its power. It had only to be forsaken to be inane, meaningless. And she knew it was meaningless. But it needed a great, passionate effort of will on the other part, seeking the colliery, still to maintain that it was meaningless.

The Rainbow, D.H. Lawrence.

We intend to sing the love of danger, the habit of energy and fearlessness. Courage, audacity and revolt will be essential ingredients of our poetry.
We affirm that the world's magnificence has been enriched by a new beauty; the beauty of speed. A racing car whose hood is adorned by great pipes, like serpents of explosive breath – a roaring car that seems to run on shrapnel – is more beautiful than the Victory of Samothrace.
We will glorify war – the world's only hygiene.
We will sing of great crowds excited by work, by pleasure, and by riot; we will sing of the multicoloured, polyphonic tides of revolution in the modern capitals. . . .

from *The First Futurist Manifesto* (1909)

1. From the first extract, discuss Ursula's perceptions of industrialization – specifically, of the colliery.
2. Look closely at Lawrence's choice of words. Consider not only Ursula's horror but also 'horrible fascination', 'swooning, perverse satisfaction in it'.
3. From the second extract, try to summarize the Futurists' attitude to mechanization.
4. Is there any commonality between their views and those of Ursula? How are they each affected by a sense of the 'power' of the machine?

Students are being introduced to the idea that different writers express different views in their attitudes towards major social changes (war, industrialization, urbanization). They are becoming aware that narrators select and shape their material and in so doing offer an interpretation of these events. It is part of the richness of literature that it allows exploration of the complexity of such issues, and studying it in the ways we are suggesting encourages students to develop an awareness of the gains as well as the losses involved in social change.

Other activities

The following examples offer further development of this idea. Students are asked to contrast the views presented (on urban and rural life) to bring out the different perspectives which the writers provide.

A.
You would not bear the dullness of the life; you don't know what it is; it would eat you away like rust. Those who have lived there all their lives, are used to soaking in the stagnant waters. They labour on, from day to day in the great solitude of steaming fields – never speaking or lifting up their poor, bent downcast heads. The hard spadework robs their brain of life; the sameness of their toil deadens their imagination; they don't care to meet to talk over thoughts and speculations, even of the weakest, wildest kind, after their work is done; they go home brutishly tired, poor creatures! caring for nothing but food and rest. You could not stir them up into any companionship, which you get in a town as plentiful as the air you breathe, whether it be good or bad – and that I don't know; but I do know, that you of all men are not one to bear a life among such labourers. What would be peace to them, would be eternal fretting to you. Think no more of it, Nicholas, I beg. Besides, you could never pay to get mother and children all there – that's one good thing.
(*North and South*, Penguin, p. 382).

B.
But heaven and earth was teeming around them, and how should this cease? They felt the rush of the sap in spring, they knew the wave which cannot halt, but every year throws forward the seed to begetting, and, falling back, leaves the young born on the earth. They knew the intercourse between heaven and earth, sunshine drawn into the breast and bowels, the rain sucked up in the daytime, nakedness that comes under the wind in autumn, showing the birds' nests no longer worth hiding. Their life and interrelations were such, feeling the pulse and body of the soil, that opened to the furrow for the grain and became smooth and supple after their ploughing, and clung to their feet with a weight that pulled like desire, lying hard and unresponsive when the crops were to be shorn away. The young corn waved and was silken, and the lustre slid along the limbs of the men who saw it. They took the udder of the cows, the cows yielded milk and pulse against the hands of the men, the pulse of the blood of the teats of the cows beat into the pulse of the hands of the men. They mounted their horses, and held life between the grip of their trees, they harnessed their horses at the wagon, and, with hand on the bridle-rings, drew the heaving of the horses after their will.
(D.H. Lawrence, *The Rainbow*, Penguin, p. 2).

C.
The breath of the manufacturing town, which made a cloudy day and a red gloom by night on the horizon, diffused itself over all the surrounding country, filling the air with eager unrest. Here was a population not convinced that old England was as good as possible.
(George Eliot, *Felix Holt*, Penguin, p. 79)

D.
. . . In this way it happened that Treby Magna gradually passed from being simply a respectable market-town . . . and took on the more complex life brought by mines and manufactures, which belong more directly to the great circulating system of the nation than to the local system to which they have been superadded; and it was in this way that Trebian Dissent gradually altered its character. Formerly it had been of a quiescent, well-to-do kind,

represented architecturally by a small, venerable, dark-pewed chapel. . . .
But when stone-pits and coal-pits made new hamlets that threatened to
spread up to the very town, when the tape-weavers came with their news-
reading inspectors and book-keepers, the Independent chapel began to be
filled with eager men and women. . . . Thus, when political agitation swept
in a great current through the country, Treby Magna was prepared to
vibrate. . . . Thus Treby Magna, which had lived quietly through the great
earthquakes of the French Revolution and the Napoleonic wars, which had
remained unmoved by the Rights of Man and saw little in Mr. Cobbett's
Weekly Register except that he held eccentric views about potatoes, began
at last to know the higher pains of a dim political consciousness.

(George Eliot, *Felix Holt*, Penguin, pp. 126–8)

E.

It was a town of red brick, or of brick that would have been red if the smoke and ashes had allowed it; but, as matters stood it was a town of unnatural red and black like the painted face of a savage. It was a town of machinery and tall chimneys, out of which interminable serpents of smoke trailed themselves for ever and ever, and never got uncoiled. It had a black canal in it, and a river that ran purple with ill-smelling dye, and vast piles of building full of windows where there was a rattling and a trembling all day long, and where the piston of the steam-engine worked monotonously up and down, like the head of an elephant in a state of melancholy madness. It contained several large streets all very like one another, inhabited by people equally like one another, who all went in and out at the same hours, with the same sounds upon the same pavements, to do the same work, and to whom every day was the same as yesterday and tomorrow, and every year the counter-part of the last and the next.

These attributes of Coketown were in the main inseparable from the work by which it was sustained; against them were to be set off, comforts of life which found their way all over the world, and elegancies of life which made, we will not ask how much of the fine lady, who could scarcely bear to hear the place mentioned. The rest of its features were voluntary, and they were these.

You saw nothing in Coketown but what was severely workful. If the members of a religious persuasion built a chapel there – as the members of eighteen religious persuasions had done – they made it a pious warehouse of red brick, with sometimes (but this only in highly ornamented examples) a bell in a bird-cage on the top of it. The solitary exception was the New Church; a stuccoed edifice with a square steeple over the door, terminating in four short pinnacles like florid wooden legs. All the public inscriptions in the town were painted alike, in severe characters of black and white. The jail might have been the infirmary, the infirmary might have been the jail, the town-hall might have been either, or both, or anything else, for anything that appeared to the contrary in the graces of their construction. Fact, fact, fact, everywhere in the material aspect of the town; fact, fact, fact, every-where in the immaterial. The M'Choakumchild school was all fact, and the school of design was all fact, and the relations between master and man were all fact, and everything was fact between the lying-in hospital and the cemetery, and what you couldn't state in figures, or show to be purchasable in the cheapest market and saleable in the dearest, was not, and never should be, world without end, Amen.

(Charles Dickens, *Hard Times*, Penguin, pp. 65–6)

Pictures that contrast in this way can be built up to stimulate discussion of a relevant theme in an A-level English Literature text. The significant point for the entitlement curriculum is that students are encouraged to see the arguments as ones about society and beliefs about society rather than as solely literary ones, and that they are aware of the kind of discussion that is involved in debating these views. In such discussions they are clarifying their own views about society and its values. As with the activities in the previous chapter, however, they uncover these attitudes and views using the traditional methods of literary criticism in the A-level classroom. One might even hope that this will give a further point to their literary studies. If students can see what can be gained by the exercise of patient, discriminating work on texts, they can see how literature develops competences not just for holding views on life, but for investigating and questioning these views.

Students' awareness of the economic, social and political concerns that bear upon the lives of individuals can be sharpened through the study of novels that are set in, and/or closely examine, specific historical periods. Of course these issues are encountered in the study of history, economics and politics at A-level, but these disciplines are less likely to provide the sense of 'felt life' than literary texts. Economic, social or political implications can be drawn out of the novel and given their own structure (as economic, political, sociological arguments). Students can then return to the text with these structures in mind, and can thus more clearly see them 'at work' through the lives of characters and the major events. It may be worthwhile, especially in a text where the economic/political issue is central, to spend some time discussing how literature differs from history/ economics, etc.

In a teaching programme at A-level on Elizabeth Gaskell's *Mary Barton*, for example, the precise nature of the perspective offered by literary study was examined in detail, as it contrasted with historical study, and as the argument of the book developed in literary terms. During the teaching programme the students were asked the following questions:

Excerpt from a teaching programme on *Mary Barton*.

1. Why can't you just copy down 'facts' from a work of literature and treat them as historical evidence?
2. In what ways can literature complement the study of history?
3. Which of the following would you expect to find in *Mary Barton*:
   (i) hard facts on numbers in the Chartist movement?
   (ii) figures on infant mortality?
   (iii) the reflection of concern for the fate of society?
   (iv) the best possible exposition of the politicians' or the economists' diagnosis?
   (v) a fairly good exposition of liberal, middle-class sympathy?
   (vi) 'the operatives' speaking in their own voice?
   (vii) a Marxist interpretation of society's ills?

   Suggest where you might look for any of the information that you wouldn't find in *Mary Barton*.

4. How does Mrs Gaskell present the relations between employer and employee in the novel?
5. From your reading of the novel, which group, operatives or employers, is presented more favourably? Can you quote from the text to support your answer? Can you suggest a reason for your answer? (i.e., why Mrs Gaskell might support one rather than the other).
6. Which member of the employer class suffers a change of heart in the book? What brings about this change? What might the author be suggesting about the future?
7. Do you think Mrs Gaskell has sympathy for the operatives – can you find some quotes to support your conclusion?
8. What's her attitude towards their turning to violence? Quote to illustrate this:
    (i) in her own words, speaking as 'the author'
    (ii) in her portrayal of the agitator brought in to talk to the men
    (iii) in the words and physical condition of John Barton as he nears the end of his life
    (iv) in the plot itself – what's the effect of the murder of Carson?
9. What kind of behaviour does Mrs Gaskell recommend to the operatives? How is this attitude shown in the literary development of the book by the portrayal, development and final situations of Alice Wilson and Margaret Legh?
10. Argue the following case, from information in the novel. Mary Barton displays some faults and has to go through punishment and ordeal before she is rewarded. Is Mrs Gaskell giving a recommendation to young ladies, and if so, what is it?
11. How many generations does the book span? In what ways do Alice Wilson and Job Legh enshrine and pass on the virtues of the old, traditional, nature-loving past? (Give examples of this.) How does Job link the old and the new by his naturalistic interests, both in terms of his methods and in his part in the book?
12. Jem is a kind of subsidiary hero in the book – how many 'heroic' acts can you find him engaged in? (Think of industrial advance as having its own kind of heroism.)
13. Does Mrs Gaskell present John Barton as a ruthless agitator or as a kind man driven to violence by his perplexities? How many examples of his social kindness do you find? Is his resort to violence clear-headed or confused? Is Mrs Gaskell sympathetic or unsympathetic to him?
14. Would you say the ending of the book reflects optimism, pessimism, or a mixture of the two about the future?

Although questions 1–3 ask students to distinguish the particular features of literature and of history, the rest of the questions preserve the discreteness of the two perspectives – economic/political interpretation and literary solution. They ask students to examine how Elizabeth Gaskell attempts to synthesize through the lives, experiences and final destinies of the characters the interconnected private and public issues. Thus, though economic, political and social issues are unmistakeably present in the novel, they are shown as part of whole lives of characters rather than as abstractions. Such a reflection on the text only adds to its value as a work of literature, because it enables students to see the nature of the contribution that literature can make to encouraging and maintaining breadth of vision in debate about social values.

Heart of Darkness

A further and even more complex example of this can be found in the novels of Conrad where explication of the issues involved must form part of the substance of the teaching itself. In *Heart of Darkness*, the issues of colonialism are inextricably related to the moral development of Marlow its narrator. This powerful short story deals not only with the ivory trade in the Congo, but with different individuals' behaviour when the conventional supports of their own society have been withdrawn.

Just how this is so can be illustrated from *Heart of Darkness*, by reflecting upon a single passage:

> You can't understand. How could you? – with solid pavement under your feet, surrounded by kind neighbours ready to cheer you or fall on you, stepping delicately between the butcher and the policeman, in the holy terror of scandal and gallows and lunatic asylums – how can you imagine what particular region of the first ages a man's untrammelled feet may take him into by the way of solitude – utter solitude without a policeman – by the way of silence – utter silence, where no warning voice of a kind neighbour can be heard whispering of public opinion? These little things make all the great difference. When they are gone you must fall back upon your own innate strength, upon your own capacity for faithfulness. Of course you may be too much of a fool to go wrong – too dull even to know you are being assaulted by the powers of darkness.
> (*Heart of Darkness*, Dent, p. 127–8).

Students might be given this passage as part of pre-reading activities on *Heart of Darkness*. They will be likely to interpret it as a comment on the supportiveness of society – the kind of passage, in other words, that might have been used as a counterweight to the 'Coketown' passage displayed above. However, by the time they reach this stage in the narrative itself they will have become aware of the irony of these observations about the protectiveness of city life. Marlow's experiences in the Congo – of inefficiency, greed, exploitation, cruelty and madness – have led him to distrust his own initially supportive code of nautical ethics. The reader realizes by this stage that the colonial lust for ivory stems from the commercial activities which form the very fabric of the 'supportive' urban life which has been described. This short story is especially rich in its recreation of the indivisibility of economic, political and social concerns and their impact on the individual life. Its central character has to abandon a simple code of ethics underpinned by convictions about the virtues of hard work and efficiency as a consequence of confronting the implications of colonial power. To survive his experiences in the Congo, Marlow is forced back upon his unsupported and isolated individual integrity. In colonial Africa, economic, political and social man is laid bare: what remains is total disintegration or a constant battle to resist corruption.

The experiences in Africa transform Marlow's robust naïveté into profound scepticism. Conrad's comment to Edward Garnett: 'Before the Congo I was only a simple animal', is paralleled by Marlow's remark to his audience, a passage which illustrates how the novelist embeds the geographical, commercial, psychological and moral within the destinies of the characters:

> It was the farthest point of navigation and the culminating point of my experience. It seemed somehow to throw a kind of light on everything about me – and into my thoughts. It was sombre enough too – and pitiful – not extraordinary in any way – not very clear either. No, not very clear. And yet it seemed to throw a kind of light.

Nostromo

The most complex treatment of the interweaving of economic, political and social themes with personal experience comes of course in *Nostromo*, focusing as it does on the European Administrador, Charles Gould's restoration of the silver mine in Sulaco to working order. The silver of this mine confronts the major characters with their private potential for corruption. The histories of the mine owner, Charles Gould, and of Nostromo, the initially free agent in the city, demonstrate the power of material interest to corrupt personal integrity; the silver whispers things to them of which they 'had no conception' and puts their secret pretences to the crucial test. Charles Gould undertakes the organization of the San Tome mine in a spirit of idealistic highmindedness: 'The mine had been the cause of an absurd moral disaster, its working must be made a serious and moral success'.

Gradually, however, Gould identifies personal prestige and his egotism with the successful working of the mine; on the mine's account he prefers to ignore the moral compromises into which he is drawn in order to make it a success. Through Charles Gould, Conrad expresses his belief in the power of the secret self to drive a man into corruptions which initially repel him, if they will further his private aims. The illusory nature of Gould's highmindedness when he becomes enmeshed in the material interests of the state are revealed thus:

> The Gould Concession had to fight for life with such weapons as could be found at once in the mire of corruption that was so universal as to lose its significance. He was prepared to stoop for his weapons. For a moment he felt as if the silver mine, which had killed his father, had decoyed him further than he meant to go; and with the roundabout logic of emotions, he felt that the worthiness of his life was bound up with success. There was no going back. (Dent, p.85)

To achieve the success which he so passionately desires, Gould allows his judgement to be 'insidiously corrupted' by the mine. He is prepared to do business with the materialist Holroyd; he backs a government doomed to failure; he becomes estranged from his wife. When we juxtapose Gould's statements against Dr. Moynagham's, whose self-distrust and consequent clear-sightedness frequently expose characters' illusions, we see the ironic light in which Conrad intends us to view the Señor Administrador's optimism. Charles Gould asserts, 'What is wanted here is law, good faith, order, security.' Dr. Moynagham, on the other hand, insists:

> There is no peace and no rest in the development of material interests. They have their law, and their justice. But it is founded on expediency, and is inhuman; it is without rectitude, without the continuity and the force that can be found only in a moral principle. Mrs. Gould, the time approaches

when all that the Gould Concession stands for shall weigh as heavily upon the people as the barbarism, cruelty and misrule of a few years back.

Events and encounters as well as direct statements reveal the gulf between Charles Gould's aspirations and the degradation into which his desire for personal success has drawn him. Forced at one stage in his political negotiations to come to terms with Hernandez, the outlawed bandit, Gould is met by an emissary who says, 'Has not the master of the mine any message to send to Hernandez, the master of the Campo?' Conrad's comment on this is:

> The truth of the comparison struck Charles Gould heavily. In his determined purpose he held the mine, and the indomitable bandit held the Campo by the same precarious tenure. They were equals before the lawlessness of the land. It was impossible to disentangle one's activity from its debasing contacts. (p. 360)

The word 'disentangle' makes the point that we have been elaborating in this chapter (or, as Curriculum Guidance on Citizenship (NCC, 1990, p. 4) put it: 'appreciate that distinguishing between right and wrong is not always straightforward'). In real life, issues are always complex and the personal and the public are always interwoven. When we ask students first to separate and then to synthesize these two strands in their literary studies, we hope that they will meet the complexities of real life with greater insight. Giving them opportunities to develop this ability to do this is, surely, part of every student's entitlement.

References

Cambridgeshire LEA (1989) Entitlement document, author.
NCC (1990) *Education for Citizenship, Curriculum Guidance No.8*, York: NCC.

CHAPTER 6

Developing a New Course: A Case-study

Communication Studies: a 'proper subject'?

When the introduction of Communication Studies was first mooted at Peter Symonds' College, there was disquiet about a subject which appeared to be nebulous and to lack intellectual rigour. A glance at the range of topics on the Communication Studies reading list seemed to confirm this. The Dewey references pointed to a dismaying diversity, with little sense of an integrated whole: Subcultures 301.44, Animal Communication 591.5 and Broadcasting 791.44/45. Part sociology, part psychology, part linguistics, with a substantial input of current affairs, Communication Studies appeared to many to offer range without depth. Objections were also raised on the grounds of its relative newness as a subject. (Communications' beginnings were marked by Shannon and Weaver's theory of communication in 1949, which arose out of their work for the Bell Telephone Company: see McQuail and Windahl, 1981.)

These suspicions were shared by parents. It had not been part of their education, and some found it difficult to see Communication Studies as a legitimate subject, while others doubted its academic rigour and had to be persuaded that it would have credibility on the UCCA form. (However, when an A grade in Communication Studies gained for one of the pilot group a place at Oxford University, the subject gained respectability in parental eyes.) To some parents it looked like a vocational course which would provide entry into, say, journalism or public relations, for students who would not have enough A-level grade points to progress to higher education. These parents had to be persuaded that this was not the primary intention of the course.

Although the course leaders could say what Communication Studies was not, they found it hard at the beginning to say what it was, and precisely what it offered students. The realization that Communication Studies is a distinct discipline came from teaching it and from observing the degree of personal growth in those students who studied it. Teachers are now, after four years, happy to assure prospective students and their parents that Communication Studies delivers significantly more than its syllabus indicates. The knowledge that it is an

A-level subject which maintains the 'gold standard' as well as providing a significant measure of entitlement is now based on very firm foundations.

Despite the uncertainties, there were compelling reasons for the inclusion of A-level Communication Studies in the A-level portfolio. The local careers advisory service had noted an increase in enquiries about careers in journalism and the media. They found that higher education courses, created during the past 10 years to cater for this demand, were attracting large numbers. These courses characteristically offered Communications elements, sometimes as a practical, sometimes as a theoretical, study. Inclusion of the course thus made sense for students wishing to proceed to higher education. However, even for students not set on entry into higher education, but still interested in a media career, the subject would clearly be of great use.

In response to these developments, senior management at Peter Symonds' College decided to introduce A-level Communication Studies into the sixth form curriculum. They had anyway already recognized that an open access college would be well advised to offer more than the traditional A-level subjects to an increasingly diverse student population. Communication Studies could offer a rewarding course to students disinclined to follow the BTEC route but unsure of their academic leanings.

A-level Communication Studies and English

Having decided to offer Communication Studies, the next problem was choosing in which department to locate it. Though its heavy reliance on visual material suggested the art department, its wide-ranging content seemed to suggest equally Psychology, Computer Studies or Social Biology. However, when process rather than content is examined, it is clear that none of these subject departments is appropriate. Dealing as it does with codes and conventions, signs and meanings, Communication Studies belongs with the study of English. Newspapers, films, television, linguistics and semiotics are all text; and therefore the natural home for Communication Studies was the English department. The skills required to explore a literary work are equally applicable and essential to the study of text in a broader context. The ability to orchestrate discussions, to introduce group work, to achieve individual response from plays, novels and poetry could be readily transferred to television programmes, comics and advertisements. Consequently, it was decided that an English specialist with experience of Communications teaching would be appointed and English department staff would form the pilot teaching groups. Where specialist skills were required, such as video-editing, provision would be made from other departments or by professionals from outside college on a visiting basis.

The decision naturally produced some nervousness in the English department. They were sure in the grasp of their own discipline, working with texts that had rested for years in substantial and well-defined library categories. Now they would be asked to deal with works from a daunting range of disciplines in their teaching of Communication Studies, disciplines with which they were not necessarily familiar. Nonetheless, the staff could see the force of the argument about process, and were prepared to pick up the challenge, secure in the knowledge that they would receive college support and practical help when they needed it. Confident that such backup was available to support them, English staff embarked on the new initiative.

Choice of examination board: AEB 608

The choice of A-level board was a much simpler matter, since the AEB is still the only board to offer a wide-ranging Communications course. Moreover, AEB 608 has a healthy pedigree, having been available since 1978. During this time, its candidature has increased steadily and now stands at over 5,000. (For a full description of the course, see Appendix 2.)

Management were thus satisfied that they were offering a course that had both academic credibility in higher education and vocational relevance; though they pointed out to prospective students that, while A-level Communication Studies was a subject relevant to a media-related degree, it would not guarantee access to it. Students taking a more directly vocational route were similarly advised: Communications might facilitate but would not guarantee entry into journalism or the media. Nonetheless, and despite this caution on the part of the staff, it is significant how many of the Peter Symonds' College students have successfully gone on to media-related degrees.

Course content

The syllabus prescribes significant processes and models of communication which the students must investigate. However, teachers have considerable flexibility to choose both particular topics and illustrative materials. The English staff took advantage of this and decided to produce a series of teaching units. The chief document was a master unit containing key concepts and relevant models for each topic. Teachers had, therefore, a checklist of materials to be covered but were free to deliver it in their own way. The assembled units were as follows:

- signs and semiotics
- mass communication – an introduction
- mass communication – organization and control
- mass media – news
- language
- groups and organizations
- technology
- interpersonal communication
- advertising and propaganda
- audiences.

Because an excellent book, *Real Images – Film and Television* (McMahon and Quinn, 1986) fulfilled the needs of teaching about film very successfully, it was decided that such a unit did not need to be manufactured. The teaching units compiled at Peter Symonds' College deal only with key concepts. For example, the language unit prescribes the key areas to be covered: what is language?;

human and animal communication; language development: functions of language; language diversity; influences on language, and the communications models relevant to these. Whilst all of these units are supported by illustrative material supplied by teaching staff, it is every teacher's responsibility to do background reading, absorb the relevant material and obtain a wider grasp of the subject. The units thus serve only as a guide to the essentials that must be covered.

It was decided that students should not have access to these units. It was felt that to allow students to have such material might limit their perspectives and give them the feeling that a grasp of a few models and key words was all they needed to know. Instead, they are encouraged to augment classroom sessions with background reading from the selection of available textbooks the department has chosen to purchase.

An advantage of the 'key units' approach is that materials for the course can be constantly updated. Staff quickly discovered that the illustrative material in media textbooks has a very short shelf-life. Whilst teachers themselves might recall Enoch Powell's 'rivers of blood' speeches in graphic detail, to 16-year-olds this event is as distant as the Punic Wars. Though it is sometimes necessary and important to give an historic perspective, for example, when discussing the history of broadcasting or of film, whenever possible all teaching should draw on the most up-to-date material available. In order to achieve this immediacy and relevance, each concept unit was accompanied by a selection of articles collected from magazines, newspapers and media publications. Frequent updating meant that students were required to observe current media and news items in terms of the theory studied in lessons. Thus every time they turned on the television or radio, theory and practice reinforced each other. Over the last three years, the Gulf War, parliamentary elections, Robert Maxwell's death, American race riots and hurricanes have all become exemplar material as soon as they have made the front page.

Whilst this makes for an exciting course which contributes significantly to the students' social and political awareness, it does put pressure on teachers constantly to update and rethink the presentation of information. However, staff think it is important that current affairs should be part of the Communication Studies classroom. The course uses theoretical concepts to explore relationships between the selection and presentation of information and prevailing social and cultural values. These links are more clearly perceived by the students if the events used to illustrate the concepts are contemporary ones. It is interesting that students can be passive viewers in front of the television in the evening, and active critics of the same programme the following day in the Communication Studies classroom.

The Communication Studies programme: organization and teaching and learning styles

Decisions then had to be made about the organization of the teaching programme. We have already described the disparate subject content of A-level Communication Studies. Delivering this content means choosing either a large number of specialist teachers (Art, Psychology, Sociology) or a small number of staff who will have to range widely across a number of disciplines. Peter Symonds' College opted for the latter course, with the proviso that, if detailed specialized knowledge were needed, this could be provided by a teacher from the relevant discipline. This decision has proved satisfactory. First, it has ensured continuity of teaching relationships with the students, particularly during the project. Second, staff have found that they have been able to make links between the initially disparate elements of the syllabus and thus give coherence and focus to the course.

Although a certain amount of the theoretical content of the course can be delivered in a didactic way in the classroom, the majority of the work lends itself to a facilitative teaching style. On a Communication Studies course, the teacher for much of the time acts as a consultant and adviser to students who are engaged on project or assignment work. Students are as likely to be in the library, the Computer Centre or other subject departments as they are to be in their timetabled room. The style of class management is very like that of the Flexible Learning programme described in an earlier chapter and is designed to promote the qualities of autonomy and self-reliance. Processes at the heart of the entitlement curriculum are thus embedded in course teaching and learning styles. Students respond well to this arrangement, which they see as a natural part of their ownership of the project or assignment on which they are engaged. They readily spend more than the allocated contact hours on their work, devoting considerable amounts of free time and homework time to their current assignments. (For staff at Peter Symonds' College, this has solved an initial timetabling problem, that of fitting extended work into the constraints of the normal school timetable.) There is a risk that, for students working largely on their own, the group might become somewhat fragmented, and to counteract this and give a sense of group identity, the policy has been to draw all the Communication Studies students together into a formal lecturing session from time to time.

Course assessment

Assessment is divided into three parts, with two final examinations and an internally assessed coursework component (the project). In one of the examinations, students are required to demonstrate their knowledge of communication theory in essay form, illustrating their answers with conceptual models. The second examination takes the form of a case-study. Before this, students are given a dossier of material to study, which may consist of newspaper articles, promotional material or pamphlets. In the examination room, students are asked to analyse this material and develop or extend it in a particular way and for a particular audience. Thus they may be asked to prepare a storyboard for a video, write a radio script, or plan a slide-and-talk show. They must then justify their choice in communications terms. This calls for the ability to assimilate factual material, to think creatively and clear-headedly under examination conditions, to select and rework information for a different audience and to select a suitable register. It is worth pointing out that few A-levels make these kinds of demands on their candidates, and indeed a former student, currently working in a radio news team, has commented on the value of preparation for this examination.

A special feature of A-level Communication Studies is the third examined component, the project, and it is here that assessment departs radically from more traditional A-levels. The project sets the student the most testing challenge. Towards the end of the first year, each student is required to identify a genuine communications need for which, over the following term, she or he has to produce a solution. An artefact must be produced, tested on a relevant audience and its effectiveness assessed. The student's work on this project is developed through the journal which she or he keeps as the work is going along. This journal is submitted with the final artefact. Students then complete their coursework by giving a talk and leading a discussion based on their work. The project can involve work in any medium the student can justify and master which is appropriate for the purpose of communication. This may involve photography, radio and audio technology, video production or the design and manufacture of written advertising or promotional material.

A-level Communication Studies and Entitlement

To begin with, sceptical English teachers at Peter Symonds' College anticipated that the content of a Communication Studies course would be transient and ephemeral in contrast to the prescribed texts for English Literature. They were apprehensive about lessons where situation comedy might be used in a study of accent; or where the first week back at college after Christmas might find students engaged in deconstructing greetings cards to determine whether the Christmas trees are 'motivated' or 'arbitrary' signs. Gradually they have come to see that, backed by a knowledge of communication theory, such pursuits go beyond the trivial. Newspaper coverage will be looked at using Gerbner's media model (McQuail and Windahl, 1981) which allows students to examine the nature of and the interplay between perception and production, whilst articles themselves will be viewed as syntagms in conjunction with their headlines, accompanying photographs and captions. (A syntagm is a combination of signs adding up to a collective meaning within an act of communication.) This is not a claim for the status of the illustrative materials used: it is an understanding of the very different status that 'texts' have in the Communication Studies classroom from their place in the English Literature classroom. What is significant in a Communication Studies course is that content illustrates theoretical perspective and is in that sense subservient to it. Students focus on processes of communication which they illustrate from material, topical or personal, that they choose or are presented with. Through this combination of theory and illustration, students develop an awareness of communication in modern society that enables them to understand it critically. In the chapter that follows, we shall examine in more detail processes of learning and course content that show the potential of the subject for delivering the entitlement curriculum.

References

McMahon, B. and Quinn, R. (1986) *Real Images – Film and Television*, Sydney: Macmillan.
McQuail, D. and Windahl, S. (1981) *Communication Models for the Study of Mass Communications*, Harlow: Longman.

CHAPTER 7

Developing Student Skills in a Variety of Media

In setting up A-level Communication Studies at Peter Symonds' College, those responsible sought ways to maximize its potential for providing entitlement. It seemed to them that the course could provide all the advantages of the 'gold standard' A-level increasingly stressed in government policy, and could also give students considerable opportunities for personal development. Indeed, closer examination of the syllabus showed that it was capable of contributing to student autonomy to a degree unmatched by any other A-level. Not only does it draw on issues relevant to the students' own life; it encourages self-determination and provides the means by which students can discover more about the nature of their society.

Transition and confidence-building

Of major and immediate importance is the ease with which A-level Communication Studies enables students to make the transition from GCSE to A-level. During this period, many students lose confidence in their ability to cope with the demands of A-level. The GCSE examination system, which has put so much emphasis on coursework and project work, has often given the students a good deal of autonomy and allowed them to express the findings of their research and ideas through a variety of responses. All too often, A-level courses leave this kind of approach behind and the requirements of major written examinations ahead turn the attention of students and their teachers, albeit unwillingly, to the hurdle of the traditional three-hour paper. Communication Studies, however, not only allows for a more sympathetic transition from GCSE to A-level, but also encourages the student to continue to respond to the demands of the course in a lively, stimulating and creative way. Indeed it can, on occasion, reward unconventionality.

Once the student realizes that he or she is not being forced into the straitjacket of essay writing, confidence can be boosted significantly. This is particularly true for many of the students who are initially attracted to the subject matter of Communication Studies. Because the ability spectrum is wide, a considerable number of those who choose Communication Studies do not see themselves as 'academic' in the traditional sense. Encouraged to stay on for educational reasons, and because of the limited availability of job opportunities post-16, these students look for subjects with which they believe they might be able to cope in terms of both content and assessment. The subject matter of Communication Studies attracts them because of its relevance and contemporaneity, and they find the assessment arrangements sympathetic, particularly since the essay component is relatively light.

The policy throughout the time Communication Studies has been offered at Peter Symonds' College has been to take advantage of these varied assessment opportunities, and to combine creative, illustrative and oral responses with essay work. In this way, students are eased relatively gently towards the three-hour written theory paper taken at the end of their second year. Also, because written responses are interspersed with projects of many different kinds, staff ensure that students have opportunities to express their knowledge and understanding in ways with which they are comfortable. Students who initially lack sophisticated writing skills are thus not disadvantaged in any way and are given time to develop these skills, while at the same time building their confidence through success in tasks undertaken in other forms.

An examination of the variety of responses made by students to set tasks over the two-year period shows how the Communication Studies department has exploited the freedom of the syllabus to draw on the wide range of skills that students bring to the course. They have produced charts and diagrams, storyboards, posters, pamphlets and questionnaires; they have written newspaper articles (complete with commissioned photographs where appropriate), written and recorded radio scripts, conducted interviews and made videos.

When the choice of response is left to the student they tend, not surprisingly, to select a medium that they enjoy handling. The confidence which this degree of choice gives students often results in pleasing evidence of their creativity. Able to use a medium congenial to them without strain, they are free to express this creativity. For example, during the study of semiotics, students were asked to prepare presentations on cultural myths which they were required to research. The teacher's expectation was that students would offer their findings in the form of an illustrated oral presentation. Two students surprised the class by jointly presenting their work in the form of a video on the theme of summer, skilfully compiled into a collage from holiday brochures, holiday photographs and television advertisements to which had been added a soundtrack. This had been researched and collated during homework periods over the course of a week and was well-received by those who saw it because of its inventiveness and vitality. The work fulfilled the requirements of the semiotics project, and at the same time involved students in using practical skills to a very high degree. The question and answer session which followed the showing enabled these students to display the oral skills which the others had demonstrated during their more conventional presentations.

From the range of strategies which students elected to adopt, it is easy to see how many of the entitlement skills of information collecting and handling are being used. Students who bring these skills to the course and extend them, or who develop skills during the course, are gaining useful competences for later life.

Moreover, the variety itself reminds us just how much information is now delivered in everyday life through media other than the written word, or rather words written in connected narrative form. The truly literate person today has to be familiar with a wide range of technological aids to communications (faxes, computers, video machines) and with an equally diverse variety of ways in which information is presented. A glance at any newspaper reminds us how often tables, charts, diagrams and questionnaires are included in articles and news items. Communication Studies students develop the ability to read-off that information for themselves rather than having to depend, as many of us do, on the information being 'translated' into connected prose. There are further points here: such 'translations' are themselves interpretations of data, and can leave room for other views, while an informed interpreter of questionnaires, especially one who has produced her or his own, can readily point to deficiencies in sampling, question-framing and the like. Thus, Communication Studies students become significantly empowered as critical receivers of information, as well as skilled creators of their own information.

Students who have thus used and mastered a range of media successfully are often more receptive to the thought that 'writing an essay' is simply another skill, not the only significant skill worth having (as many other A-levels imply by their assessment requirements). Much of the anxiety is thus removed. For Communication Studies students, essay-writing skills are developed during the revision period leading up to the examinations. By this time the theoretical elements of the course have been absorbed, so that students are not grappling with complex ideas at the same time as they are trying to put them on paper. Their enthusiasm for practising essay skills is sustained before the examinations by a lucky dip of questions ranging over the whole course. Students write on the topics which fall to them, and are free to write on as many issues as they choose. Indeed, this strategy seems to generate so much enthusiasm for essay writing that the demands on teachers for marking and feedback are quite significant.

Group work and pair work: theory and practice

Developing students' confidence is a central aim of the entitlement curriculum. Staff at Peter Symonds' College discovered that confidence was fostered from the very beginning of the course by group and pair work. Since group theory is part of the syllabus, students not only have the opportunity to work collaboratively, but are also invited to examine their practices in the light of their increasing knowledge of group dynamics. For example, a camera might be placed in the room to allow them to examine their own participation in group situations. Thus a kind of symbiosis develops between theory and practice. Individual confidence is also encouraged in the first terms through a study of intrapersonal and interpersonal communication. It is significant that at Peter Symonds' College, A-level Communication Studies shares popularity with A-level Psychology. It seems likely that both subjects promise in part an exploration of self at a time when the young person's developing sense of personal identity and relationship to the rest of the world is particularly important. That such study is part of Communication Studies becomes clear to the students at an early stage of the course through a practical investigation. Very soon after they begin the course they are asked to construct a circle of influence in which they examine their own decision to come to college, and try to estimate the importance of the factors which have contributed to their choice of action. Very often students have given little serious consideration to decision-making processes in their own life. Through this investigation, however, they see that social and cultural factors have already played a significant part in their existing attitudes, values and beliefs. This serves as an initial, often challenging, introduction to an understanding of self and society. However, the greatest contribution which the interpersonal component makes to entitlement is that it gives the student a theoretical basis from which to manage social interaction. The knowledge that social skills are not used merely in leisure and party situations, but are employed in all encounters with other people, comes as a surprise to most students. Through role-play and television interviews, they are made aware of the importance of listening, of interpreting the body language of others, of responding to feedback, of giving signs of approval.

An interesting variation on the opportunities given to students to come to terms with the values of the world in which they live is provided by a study of non-verbal communication, the culmination of which is a visit to the Museum of Mankind. The brief undertaken there is to examine how role is conveyed through head-dress. In this project, students are encouraged to express their answer in the form of illustrations with written commentary. Far from being seen as an anthropological study with little relevance to themselves, it proves to be very fruitful, as students are then able to transfer what they have learned from tribal regalia to their own lives and to follow this up by an equivalent study of the insignia of their own society's groups and structures.

A-level Communication Studies and media study

Treatment of the media often features in General Studies courses or Current Affairs sessions. But the drawback such presentations have is that, because of time constraints on the syllabus, they tend to be occasional and of short duration. Also, like all 'additionality' programmes, they can be seen as less important by students.

In the Communication Studies syllabus, however, study of the media is a major topic, requiring an historical and analytical examination of radio, television and the press. Students are therefore obliged to scrutinize the operation of the media in close detail, work which is supplemented throughout by continuous reference to contemporary events. This work relates theory to practice, academic study to the outside world, and builds students' confidence in their ability to make intelligent and informed comments about the way information is processed. Students come to their course with a comprehensive knowledge of television programmes and some familiarity with the tabloid press, but few of them have any idea at all about how these came into being or their history. This is not really surprising: after all, few of the A-level English Literature students come to texts with a knowledge of literature and its symbols and origins. However, in the case of the Communication Studies students, there is a deeper point. In their largely uncritical acceptance of the content of television and radio programmes and newspaper articles as truth, they show a lack of awareness of the selecting, shaping and biasing techniques that have gone on before the images or the words are presented to them. The function of the media as both reflector and promoter of society's values has hardly occurred to them.

First steps in media study

Rather than plunge students into theoretical discussion of the media, they are gently eased into the topic. First lessons on media are taken up with challenging some of their assumptions about television. For example, they tend to believe that entertaining programmes have no further effect other than amusement. An exercise which alerts them to this is one in which members of a class are asked to collect words which bring to mind 'Australia'. This they do readily, creating long lists in which 'billabongs' and 'barbies' proliferate. A headcount usually reveals that no more than two members of the class have been to Australia or have any direct contact with anyone having knowledge of the country. Very quickly they realize that their picture of Australia has been constructed from an amalgam of feature films, soap operas, television comic acts, advertisements and travelogues. They are starting to develop an awareness of how the media creates and then confirms their attitudes and opinions. As the course develops, students recognize that those who have access to the media have access to an important instrument of control.

Developing awareness of the media

Once they have seen the power of the media to shape their perceptions, students are asked to consider the portrayal in the media of certain groups, to assess their 'visibility' or 'invisibility' and thus their importance, as the media world sees it. They are asked particularly to be observant about the contexts within which these groups are shown. In the following activity, students are asked to carry out the research and compare findings.

Lesson plan 1: Women in television programmes

1. Make a headcount of men and women appearing on TV during a single evening's viewing.
2. Note whether programmes which feature women have a different type of content/story from those which feature men.
3. Observe how men and women are portrayed in situation comedy – do you find evidence of stereotyping? (Give examples.)
4. What kinds of products are women most likely to advertise?
5. Keep a tally of how many male, and how many female, voice-overs are used in advertisements and say for what kind of products they are used.
6. Find out how often female sport is featured on TV.
7. Observe any examples of male bias in language.

Lesson plan 2: Stereotypes in soap operas

After watching an episode of 'Coronation Street', write the script for a 5-minute radio programme which takes a critical look at this programme. Your target audience is not 'Coronation Street' watchers. Your script should try to address the following:

- What impression might the programme create about the North of England for a South of England viewer?
- How does it represent the world of work?
- What roles does it ascribe to women?
- What use does the programme make of dialect, redundancy and restricted codes?
- Attempt a semiotic analysis of its opening title sequence.
- How does the programme use symbolic codes?
- How representative is the casting of the actual population of urban Lancashire?

Students are encouraged to develop this work in ways they find interesting. The course offers them opportunities to carry out more detailed investigation of situation comedy and soap operas. Apart from extending the exploration of the portrayal of women, this also reveals to them how, in the media, the nuclear family is still the benchmark of family life. (Though self-contained at the time, such findings can later be linked to work on newspapers, when students come to discuss in detail the economic norms in society and their links with the media.) With remarkable regularity, students who have made these investigations as part of a communications project state that they will never again read a newspaper or watch a programme on TV with quite the same degree of passive acceptance. By their own account, this kind of teaching, delivered within an A-level rather than as an enforced addition to the timetable, gives them perspectives which they continue to hold after they have left college. It does not seem to alter their viewing patterns; what it does is to give them a kind of 'critical literacy' that lets them distance themselves from the media and see the nature and purpose of the material put before them.

Broadening the context of media study

As has been made clear, television programmes and newspapers form a major area of study in this A-level and by this means students are invited to take a critical and well-informed look at their own society. Once they have been made aware of the history of broadcasting and of the press, they are invited to identify the particular characteristics of a variety of newspapers. This is best done in twos, answering a list of questions and then giving feedback to the rest of the class in the form of a talk with overhead projections. A series of questions such as the following keeps the research focused:

1. Who owns the newspaper?
2. Who advertises in the newspaper, and what proportion of the newspaper is given over to advertisements?

3. Establish different categories of news and say what proportions of the newspapers is devoted to each of these.
4. Can you identify the political affiliations of the newspaper?

This work is now extended when students are asked to undertake further research. As with previous work on representations of people in soap operas, comedies and sport, students are asked again to move their investigations outwards from the self. To do this, an activity is created with which they may feel some empathy. The following story is presented to them:

Lesson plan 3: Reporting news

On Saturday, December 16, a party was held at 34 Heaney Close, Westchester, for Miss Samantha Hinton's 18th birthday. Mr and Mrs Hinton were abroad in the Canary Islands at the time, but had given their permission for Samantha to entertain her friends that night. At about 1 a.m., neighbours concerned about the number of partygoers in the quiet residential area, alerted the police. At 1.15 a.m., three police cars arrived at the four-bedroomed house, where about 200 teenagers, mostly students from a local college, were gathered.

Police attempted to restore order and in the process of arresting students who were in a disorderly state, a 16-year-old boy, Gary Martin, was shot. Gary died an hour later at Westchester General Hospital of a bullet wound in the chest. Mr and Mrs Martin, parents of the dead boy, said that they had no idea that he was at the party. To their knowledge, he did not know Samantha Hinton, and was not a member of her circle. He was a pupil at a local comprehensive school and had never been in any trouble before.

Mr Martin, a local property developer and member of the Town Council, said that he intended to instigate an enquiry into the events. The local chief of police, Chief Inspector Richardson, expressed his concern and stated that a police investigation would be held in order to establish why firearms had been used. This was not normal police practice.

The class is divided into groups with each group working for a different organization: local weekly newspaper; Radio 1; local radio, *The Daily Telegraph*, *The Daily Mirror*, *The Daily Mail*, ITV and News at Ten. The story above, they are told, has come from a news agency. Using their knowledge of the medium they represent, each group is asked to construct a news item based on the material. They must select the political stance which would be most likely adopted, determine the appropriate register, commission a photograph, write a caption and create headlines. Students have to be astute and discriminating in recreating the tone of their particular news medium. Also, the project calls for a number of responses both written and oral, as well as encouraging some students to use storyboarding in creating their News at Ten item.

Lesson plan 4: World news

Students now embark on a close study of the presentation of news itself. This draws their attention not only to economic interests in society but also to the extent to which news bulletins on TV and radio can reflect and foster the attitudes, values and beliefs of particular societies.

The object of this lesson is two-fold. First, it is to familiarize students with the concept of 'news value'. Second, it is to demonstrate that the world news on the national network is meaningful only to a particular society.

In the previous week's lesson, staff instruct students to begin monitoring BBC Nine o'clock and ITV Ten o'clock News. They should make a record of each evening's items and note the running order. If they are unable to watch these, they should video them and run them through fast later. It needs to be emphasized to students that they are not doing an in-depth survey, merely collecting the headlines.

At the beginning of the media lesson, divide students into groups of four or five. Ask them to compare notes and to categorize their findings. What kind of items receive the fullest coverage? Is there a noticeable order of priority in these items? (Allow about 15 minutes for this.)

Now give each group a list of news items, such as the following:

- Earthquake in Central America – 20 dead.
- Inner city riot in Liverpool – five youths arrested.
- Duke of Edinburgh snubs Japanese ambassador.
- Child vanishes from caravan site – police hunt man in Ford Escort.
- Albanian refugees face winter of starvation.
- Unemployment figures reach 3 million.
- National Curriculum debated at NUT Conference.
- Madonna collapses at Wembley Stadium concert.
- European Community calls for legislation on pig farming.
- Prime Minister flies to Washington for summit conference.

Using the information they have gathered from their monitoring of genuine bulletins, students are asked to establish a running order for these items on the Nine o'clock News (the items can be updated as required). (Give 10–15 minutes for this.)

Bring the class together for feedback on their answers. Ask them to establish the most popular running order. This will produce discussion and argument, and will focus attention on the idea that what counts as 'news' is not fixed.

Using an OHP or flip-chart, remind students of the list of 'news values': 'frequency', 'threshold', 'unambiguity', 'meaningfulness', 'consonance', 'unexpectedness', 'continuity', 'composition', 'reference to élite nations', 'reference to élite persons', 'personalization' and 'negativity'. Ask students to award points to items depending on how many 'news values' they contain.

Return students to original groups. Each group is to act as a news team from a particular country – USA, Malawi, Argentina, Australia, Germany, Poland. They are also told that the news items on the list have been received by them from Reuters. The group is asked to decide which, if any, of these items they will include in their own country's 9 o'clock news. (Five minutes for this.)

Re-convene the class and ask groups to compare their selections. If the list of countries is wide, there should be an interesting set of responses. This exercise can lead to work on news-gathering and gate-keeping, or can be used as an introduction to work on the values of our own society.

Having identified such a focus in news presentation, students are then encouraged to do in-depth media surveys on the presentation of any sub-group (women, old people, the disabled, ethnic minorities) in newspapers, TV and film. Students are asked to range as widely as possible in their choice of material and include sport, entertainment programmes and advertising, as well as serious news reporting. Their investigations show that the representation of their chosen sub-group will vary according to the kind of programme: a group may be 'invisible' to advertisers if it is not thought to have selling appeal; a group may be portrayed as funny and lovable in entertainment programmes but difficult and obstreperous in news reporting. More importantly, building on the media work they have done, students can account for these variations in presentation. They can now see that they have been observing how bias operates on different levels, that it exists not only within separate media organizations, but is part of an overall ideological standpoint that can be associated with the American, European, male-centred view of the world.

The media: ownership and control

Students can go on to further work on ownership and control in the media. Given information about ownership of radio and TV stations, satellite and cable broadcasting, newspapers, magazines, films, records and publishing, they are asked to provide a visual representation of ownership: in short, to answer in more detail the question, 'Who owns what?'. This exercise alerts students to the extent to which public opinion is controlled by powerful organizations and individuals. Students debate whether there should be public service broadcasting or whether the media should be controlled by economic factors. Made aware of these vested interests, students can continue to question what is put before them in their adult lives.

Advertising and propaganda: the ethical question

The object of this lesson is to raise students' awareness of the role of advertising in society. Plenty of advertising material should be available in the class, from *Exchange and Mart* to glossy full-colour supplements.

Tell students that they have two kittens to sell quickly and that they need to construct an advertisement for the local paper which guarantees that the kittens will be highly sought after. In turn, students read their advertisements to the rest of the class. Most will emphasize the kittens' cuteness and fluffiness; some will use humour.

Now point out to the class that these kittens might be unattractive, smelly and destructive. Could they still advertise in the ways they have suggested if they know this to be the case? This stimulates a discussion about the ethics of advertising. The class can then be divided into two groups; one to decide the arguments which can be put forward in favour of effective advertising irrespective of truth, and one to develop arguments that stress the importance of veracity. A group activity such as this is likely to produce the following arguments:

- advertising gives choice; provides information; makes for economies of scale; creates employment;
- advertising encourages a wasteful society; leads to the creation of false needs; diverts manufacturers from producing items which arise out of real need.

Bring class together and compare notes.

Continue this work by using selected examples of advertising, ranging from the strictly informative to the 'hard sell'. Encourage students to examine some advertising material using semiotics to discuss their findings.

Exercises such as this can lead to lessons on the parallels between advertising techniques and propaganda.

Advanced communications technology

The prime purpose of this area of teaching is to give students sufficient insight into contemporary developments for them to be able to reflect on both the philosophical implications and the aesthetic aspects of advanced communications technology. Some of the ways in which communications technology impinges on their lives will already be evident to them. Early in the course, they will have charted their own listening and viewing patterns and those of their families. Few, however, will be aware in any detail of other features of communications technology and their impact on individuals and wider society.

Task 1: Technology in your personal life

Chart an imaginary but typical 24 hours in your life. Record all occasions on which you come into contact with communications technology (begin when you wake up, switch off alarm, switch on radio . . .). This exercise draws their attention to the range and diversity of communications technology which impinges on their lives. Their lists are likely to include local and national radio, TV news and satellite football, bank cards, research in school library and hired videos.

Task 2: Technology in the public domain and the speed of change

(a) Interview a member of your family or an acquaintance older than yourself. Enquire whether he or she thinks advances in communications technology have had any effects on their life. (These might include insignificant instances like booking cinema tickets.)

(b) Discover 10 different occupations directly concerned with communications technology. (These might include air traffic controllers and Visa card processors.)

Discussion – benefits and threats

Students will already be thinking about contentious issues during their work on media. What might have been uncritically seen as entirely beneficial aspects of technology now begin to be questioned. For example, they see some of the drawbacks of the following: centralized information records, increased and instantaneous news coverage, and the breakdown of cultural barriers. What follows are examples of the issues students are encouraged to discuss:

1. Is it advantageous to society to have a population with compulsory identity cards?
2. Will increased speed of communication favourably affect all aspects of our lives or will it put increased pressure on people unused to the stresses of a faster working pace?
3. How might Third World countries fare as First World countries increase the level of sophistication of their own technology?
4. Does advanced communication technology iron out or accentuate national differences?
5. Should institutions to whom you give details about yourself have the right to sell such information to other organizations?
6. What are the implications for a country's laws and culture when satellite programmes can be beamed in from outside their areas of jurisdiction?
7. How do you think the broadcasting of stock market figures might affect the economies of other countries?
8. What kind of effect on society might arise from a greater number of people working from home?
9. How will retailing practices be altered by home shopping?
10. What might be the effect of instant news coverage during a war?

Task 3: Taking control of technology

1. Research some aspect of communications technology in order to obtain the most up-to-date information. Areas you might investigate include: recorded music, broadcasting, printing, aspects of computer technology, telephones, shopping.
2. Organize a programme the day before an election to maximize the chances of a prospective parliamentary candidate. Indicate where and which technology might be employed.
3. Consider the implications for society of increased communications technology. Do you feel that it promises a new kind of Utopia or does it in your view portend Dystopia? In groups record a five-minute radio item which examines the subject from one or the other point of view.

A series of tasks such as these will have alerted students to the significance of the degree of control that technology exerts over their lives. The tasks will also have made them aware that the expectation of instantaneous information demands increasingly sophisticated communications technology.

The concept of entitlement 16–19 has sharpened all teachers' awareness of the critical understanding that students need if they are to function in adult life as independent-minded individuals. We have argued in this chapter that, in addition to the high-order skills (analysis, synthesis, logical presentation) developed by traditional A-level courses, students need an understanding as well as a degree of control over advanced technology. The Communication Studies syllabus satisfies these requirements, giving students opportunities to theorize at a high level as well as to gain familiarity with and a critical perspective on the technological aspects of society today.

From the study of the media and of technology, and from the topic areas considered within them, the reader will see how many of the thematic areas of the entitlement curriculum take their place quite naturally in the Communication Studies course. Social, political and economic issues are at the heart of its concerns, with ample opportunity to illustrate these in matters of equal opportunity, environmental awareness and education for citizenship. The entitlement curriculum and the Communication Studies syllabus share the same beliefs about processes and content.

CHAPTER 8

The Communication Studies Project: Autonomy and Critical Awareness

This chapter describes and illustrates the central role of the project in Communication Studies. After several years' experience of the syllabus teachers are convinced that in the course of preparing and presenting their projects, Communication Studies students develop a high degree of personal autonomy. Earlier chapters have indicated how independent decision-making is encouraged throughout the course, but it is the project above all that develops and extends this process. Throughout the extended period of planning, justifying, researching, collating and recording that go into producing the project, students must make their own decisions at each stage. It is their project, about which they know more than anyone else, so they alone can manage it. Work on the project, then, could fairly be said to be the entitlement curriculum in action.

From the processes outlined above, it can be seen that the project makes heavy demands on students. Even after the lengthy business of finding a genuine communication need, the *sine qua non* of any project, students are obliged to use quite sophisticated social and technical skills: they have to learn how to approach organizations and individuals in ways that will produce the information they wish, then they have to process and present these findings in appropriate ways. Valuable lessons have been learned by Communication Studies teachers at Peter Symonds' College as they have looked for the best ways to prepare students for the demands of the project. The first model was to set up a skills course in the second half of the summer term for the lower sixth. The idea was to equip students with the skills they would need for the successful presentation of their project. Thus they were trained in word-processing, video production and editing, photography and presentation skills. This, it was thought, would remove much of the worry about methods of presentation and the final 'performance', and leave the students free to concentrate upon developing the content of their project.

To the surprise of the staff, these courses were not entirely successful: students saw the course as rather pointless, and unrelated to any significant activity on which they were engaged. Even though staff assured them that they would need these skills for the successful completion of the project, students' response remained lacklustre.

It was clear that a different strategy would have to be adopted. After much discussion, staff opted for the setting of a 'mini-project': staff compiled a number of short research tasks each of which fulfilled a genuine communication need. Students were invited to choose a topic from this list and to complete the task over six weeks in private study and free time. The following examples are representative of the tasks that staff devised:

1. Many people are anxious to find accommodation close by for elderly relatives. Can you compile a guide to all the available residential care in your home town? Intended audience – people of your parents' age who have old people to care for.
2. What play groups and nursery schools has your town to offer? Intended audience – local parents of small children.
3. Can you compile a guide for those planning to learn to drive and prepare information about applying for a licence? Intended audience – all students approaching their seventeenth birthday.
4. Can you devise a fool-proof guide to the college computer network? Intended audience – students not yet computer literate and nervous of the equipment.
5. The Adult Education Centre requires publicity material for its one-year A-level courses commencing in September. Intended audience – the general public.

Staff were aware that this piece of research, though small-scale, would add to the students' already considerable load, but the experiment has proved extremely successful in a number of ways. Whilst many students felt initial trepidation at having to work entirely on their own, they quickly developed a sense of 'ownership' of their task. As they felt the need to develop a particular technical skill, they asked for appropriate help from staff at the college; since time was limited they found themselves becoming more aware of the need for effective self-management. The sense of achievement in completing a whole task on their own gave students encouragement about the main project. Finally, this initial experience of contacting outside organizations and members of the public gave them confidence for the larger-scale work that lay ahead.

Support from the college enhanced the students' sense of achievement. Not only was appropriate technical help provided when it was requested, but the artefacts produced by the students were shown to be valued by the college: posters and pamphlets were displayed, and in some cases put into use by the college as part of its own promotional material.

It is worth reflecting on the lessons learned by the staff here. The skills-based course looked attractive and potentially useful, but it was unsuccessful with the students. Yet they requested the same skills when engaged on their mini-project. The clear lesson is that motivation to develop and employ a range of practical skills arises best from the natural demands of a task rather than from a stand-alone instructional course.

The project

In the course of the mini-project, students are encouraged to think about possible topics for their main project, and once they have identified a topic they sign a 'contract' with the department. During the summer between the lower and upper sixth they begin to collect data and contact appropriate organizations. During this time they are on their own, and this is their first sustained period of individual decision-making about their project. When they get back to college in September they can encounter their first setbacks. It may turn out that their chosen area has already been covered, and/or no genuine communication need exists, or their proposed study is too ambitious. These difficulties must be resolved through negotiation with their tutors after which they proceed to the first stage of the extended study.

Aspects of the project

Rationale: students must provide a written justification of the processes undertaken to determine that a communication need exists which they can fulfil. This calls for considerable analytical skill. The distinctive feature of this important preparatory work is that students are applying analytical skills to materials of their own creation rather than to set texts.

Relationship between teacher and student

Unlike project work undertaken as an assessed component in other A-levels, Communication Studies offers students the opportunity to range widely in almost any direction. Since the onus for the project is upon the student, this means that the teacher/supervisor is not necessarily in an informed position concerning the topic undertaken and the student thus has considerably more input than in the usual pupil/teacher situation. Though it may seem that the teacher is little more than a sounding board, those students who regularly consult their supervisor invariably do better than those who work entirely alone.

Staff teaching A-level Communication Studies at Peter Symonds' College have developed more of a facilitative role since they started teaching the subject. They work with students on such matters as defining achievable project topics, setting targets for the work, advising on approaches to institutions, and shaping the final presentation.

The journal

The journal is an important part of the project, providing a record of all the research that the student carries out as it is being done. It thus deals with the students' attempts to collect data, and his or her reflections upon the success of this, analysed in terms of communications theory. The journal also records skills already acquired and skills needed to complete the project. The journal is, therefore, a record of personal and social development over a period of nearly six months, and ranges reflectively over students' achievements, current concerns and future plans in an honest and open way. The part the journal plays in the student's entitlement is highly significant, since it becomes a substantial exercise in self-assessment, and thus contributes to the larger college record of achievement process that every student has to undertake.

The following advice is given to students about the journal.

Theory in your journal

There are no strict rules. It is important that all theory is actually based on your own observation, research, design and thought. It shouldn't be stuck on like lego bricks but grow from your work naturally. Having said this, it is still true that good journals are characterized by intelligently applied theory and you should be aiming to do this whenever relevant and appropriate.

Think of the following areas:

Design:
semiotics, semantic differential, etc., to be used in analysing your products.

Comparative and stimulus materials:
all to be fully analysed. Use both language theory (register, dialect, appropriateness, etc.) and image analysis (film and semiotics).

Own language:
spoken (interviews, surveys, presentations) and written (journal, letters, reports, artefact). Explain choice of style, register, dialect, etc.

Models:
construct your own and adapt from those you've been given. Use them to illuminate what you think is important in any piece of communication.

Interpersonal:
factors like perception, feedback, channel, etc. Examine your artefact and individual elements of your project like interviews, surveys or lessons observed.

Groups and organizations:
are you working with any? Show how the dynamics and structures influence the communication you are involved in.

Representation:
be aware of the way you construct representations of reality in your artefact. Show that you are aware of the images of gender, ethnic groups, class and age that you use.

NVC:
show that you are in control of this and that you are aware of how others are using it. Use theory to explain what happens, i.e., halo effect.

Surveys:
have you collected genuine statistical evidence to support your work?

Audiences:
be very clear about exactly who your audience is and how you are intending to work with it. Will Effects Theory be useful?

Technical skills:
> are you learning new skills? Give full details and don't pretend you are an instant expert.

Above all, there are four key elements in a good journal:

Describe what you have done.
Reflect on why you did it and how well you did it.
Analyse why it happened the way it did.
Learn from this what you will do next.

Your journal must be well organized and easy to use. Remember that the people who mark it won't have any background knowledge of you or your project. The journal must also be attractive and inviting. Avoid page after page of solid text by using diagrams, illustrations, lists and sketches.

Time management

Students learn about this in a number of ways. First, there is the obvious point that the period of time for the project, which seemed to stretch before them at the end of the lower sixth year, suddenly narrows alarmingly as October, and the final weeks for completion of the project, arrives. Then, as they prepare their final artefact, they often find that they still need to improve on presentation and preparation skills and have not allowed sufficient time for this. A further aspect of time management, however, provides yet another example of how theory and practice meet in the Communication Studies syllabus. During the previous term, students had studied group and organizational theory, and examined the nature of bureaucracy. They discover during research for the project the practical implications of this theory as some of their letters go unanswered, some of their telephone calls go unreturned, and they encounter many delays as they try to arrange interviews. Under such circumstances they discover the importance of planning.

Financial constraints

At first, Communication Studies staff were concerned that the limited amount of college equipment would hamper student creativity and perhaps jeopardize the final success of some projects. In practice, however, this turned out not to be the case: students saw this as just another problem for them to solve, and either worked out ways to share college equipment or used considerable inventiveness to find other means of representing their findings. For the individual student, the cost incurred in producing the artefact often provides a further learning experience. Usually this is because the student significantly underestimates the cost of producing the range of supporting material (posters, pamphlets, education packs). Sometimes this can have its humorous side, as in the case of the boy who designed and produced a poster to encourage students to dispose of soft drinks cans neatly and tidily. 'Crush it, bin it' his poster proclaimed: but when his fellow students dutifully tried to put their squashed cans into the collecting bins they found the aperture too narrow: a clear, but costly, case of insufficient market research.

The project and the entitlement curriculum

The processes involved in researching, preparing and presenting the project give students opportunities to develop many of the skills and competences proposed in policy statements about entitlement. Students are involved in communications with a wide range of organizations and individuals and as a consequence they develop beneficial social and personal skills. As they develop their ideas, they have to make decisions and solve problems in real, rather than artificial situations. Their information collecting often requires skills of numeracy and presentation which extend their use of technology.

These processes are common experiences for all students on Communication Studies courses. However, if we turn to the range of topics that students undertake to investigate, it is clear that the project contributes significantly to themes and issues of the entitlement curriculum: equal opportunities, citizenship, health education, visual/aesthetic awareness, environmental awareness, are all represented in the investigations carried out by Peter Symonds' College students.

We have pointed out that students are free to research any aspect of communications that interests them, as long as they can demonstrate a genuine communication need. Nonetheless, it is interesting to note how often the topic chosen indicates a real degree of social commitment on the student's part. The following list is representative of the topics chosen by Communication Studies students.

1. Claire chose to create an anorexia awareness lesson pack for use with fifth formers. During her GCSE final year, a friend had suffered from the disease and was hospitalized. Claire's research shows that had her peer group had more information on the illness, they would have been able to alert the authorities to their classmate's plight at an earlier stage and perhaps alleviate some of her physical and psychological suffering. (Entitlement area – Health Education.)
2. Natalie, a competent and enthusiastic ballet dancer who planned to study the subject at college, was aware that more females are attracted to ballet than males. Knowing that it would provide good exercise for males as well as increasing the number of potential male dancers, she decided to alter the popular perception of ballet as a female activity and attempt to recruit boys for her ballet school. (Entitlement area – Equal Opportunities.)
3. Paul, an enthusiastic driver, decided to offer students a guide to motor insurance, car tax and post-accident procedure, as his research revealed that his peer group was lamentably ill-informed. (Entitlement areas – Economic Understanding, Citizenship.)
4. Nick, a keen golfer, was aware that golf clubs were surrounded by an aura of superiority and often intimidated young players who might have wished to join. He chose to explain the ins and outs to would-be members. (Entitlement area – Equal Opportunities.)
5. Simon, having had an ileostomy, decided to provide information for students

in college about the disease. His research led him to discover that the Ileostomy Association was interested in his producing a support package for young people who were to undergo the operation themselves. (Entitlement area – Health Education.)

The significant factor about all the projects mentioned here is that they all involve the students in topics they know and understand. However, in every case they had to adopt a new focus: taking an objective stance, interviewing senior officials or canvassing interested parties. Moreover, some students looked outside their immediate area of interest:

7. Trevor came into contact with a struggling pop group which could not afford to make a professional video to accompany the single with which they planned to break into the music world. Trevor fulfilled this need and was delighted when it was shown on television. (Entitlement areas – Visual/aesthetic awareness, Equal Opportunities.)
8. Tania learnt that the local Adult Basic Education centre was insufficiently advertised. Working in conjunction with her local organization, she designed posters and recorded a local radio programme to promote the classes. (Entitlement areas – Visual/aesthetic awareness, Citizenship.)
9. David discovered that a local organization was fighting the Ministry of Transport over a controversial road-building policy. He designed T-shirts and screenprinted them to give visible group identity to the protesters. Campaigners were subsequently seen wearing the T-shirts in news photographs. (Entitlement areas – Visual/aesthetic awareness, Citizenship.)

The range of entitlement areas covered in this list is wide. Impressively, nearly all the projects have at their heart a socially useful outcome, either some distinct benefit to a group or the general raising of awareness about an issue. Communication Studies staff hope that the benefits of channelling adolescent enthusiasm and idealism in such socially useful directions will last beyond the students' college years into adult life: an aim shared, of course, by advocates of the entitlement programme.

A project illustrated

To show, finally, how skills and issues fuse in the work of a student, we let a typical Communication Studies student speak in her own voice.

The following annotated extracts are taken from Aline's project undertaken at Peter Symonds' College during 1990–91. Aline is quoted extensively to show how students engaged on a project are able to reflect on their acquisition of skills and upon the stages through which they pass as they plan, research and write their project.

Aline's justification of need begins thus:

> The idea for my project evolved as I have been working for a year at McDonalds on a part-time basis and since I have been there I have received a significantly high number of customer complaints regarding environmental issues. An extreme example of one situation I faced was when three 15- or 16-year-old females entered our Eastleigh store producing a petition signed

by around 50 students. The petition demanded McDonalds show environmental awareness.

Aline then began two investigations, first into McDonalds' environmental policy and then into the public's perceptions of the company. This involved her in carrying out a survey of the company's advertising material, their in-store fact sheets and their full-page environmental awareness promotion in *The Independent*. She then carried out a survey of young people's attitudes to the company through questionnaires and made a statistical analysis of the resulting information. Despite McDonald's efforts it seemed that few saw them in a favourable light.

> I arranged a personal interview with the manager of Eastleigh McDonalds store in order to discuss the environmental situation with him.

Evidence was collected from newspapers in which McDonalds' ranching policy in Central and South America came under critical examination.

> Letters that I have sent off to environmental groups have given me more support to my theory that the public regard McDonalds as an environmentally destructive company. The research that I have collected: questionnaires, interviews, observation, experts' views, newspaper and magazine cuttings, etc., strongly show clear evidence to support the view that despite all McDonalds' publicity, evidence indicates that teenagers between the ages of 14 and 18 do not see McDonalds as an environmentally friendly company. Therefore I propose McDonalds' publicity as it stands is not getting through to its targeted audience.

> The aim of my project therefore will not be to redesign McDonalds' publicity campaign in the hope of altering students' opinions, but to tackle the problem from a different angle altogether. I will produce and test out a boardgame and try it out on primary school age children to educate them on green issues. Incorporated in this boardgame will be McDonalds shown as an active company in saving the world and as doing the best it can to preserve the world their customers live in.

Aline went on a county youth band tour of Canada that summer where she continued her research in order to determine whether her local perception of McDonalds was an international one. The same negative attitude to the company prevailed. From Quebec to Toronto she visited 20 different McDonalds in pursuit of information.

> To concentrate my Canadian research findings I suggest it is not just British people who have formed the idea of an 'uncaring' McDonalds but it is present in the Canadian society too. Could this be a worldwide communication problem?

Back in England, Aline set up a series of interviews and telephone calls in order to gain information. After her call to the head of the company's public relations department in London, Aline commented:

> After this phone call I felt even better and felt I had achieved something positive towards my project. I realize I am gaining an ability to communicate well with people in authority and am pleased with my progress in this area.

Aline then visited her local library and collected the names of 11 environmental organizations to which she then wrote. At the same time she continued her analysis of McDonald's own public material and followed her comments with this reflection:

> I am finding from doing this project that it is helping my communication skills as I am learning to analyse different material in various ways and put my communication models and theories into practical use,

and a little later:

> I have learnt so far about many problems of interpersonal communication especially in the form of letters. I am pleased with the way I am managing phone calls, interviews, consultations and letters.

Aline then began to work on the boardgame with which she hoped to change the adverse perceptions of McDonalds which might already be held by 8-year-olds. She began by examining the range of education boardgames already available in the shops. This was then followed by an interview with a teacher of 8-year-olds from whom she gleaned information about their ability level. She then 'borrowed' neighbours' children in order to find out how much they knew about environmental concerns.

At this juncture she was asked to give a talk to the class on the progress of her project and commented:

> I was extremely nervous to do this in front of nine people! And I knew them! I understand however that this will help me to prepare and carry out my final oral presentation for my project, but the experience was still terrifying. I was pleased with the mark I achieved however, a B, and this has encouraged me to do well in my final oral presentation. I learnt from this the need to plan effective notes to stop me from forgetting or running out of things to say, of getting confused and lost on the way.

The following weeks were devoted to creating the boardgame which contained jungle images, the McDonalds logo and question and answer cards on environmental concerns. This was tested on school children at appropriate intervals and analysed using communication theory. In December, Aline recorded that, 'It has taken me two months to produce the final boardgame and I am pleased with the result'.

In the following February, Aline tested her boardgame by taking it along to a primary school and getting 7- and 8-year-olds of mixed ability and both sexes to play it. She then evaluated the success of the game and its potential for changing perceptions of McDonalds.

Her final self-assessment indicates how she regarded her own performance throughout. Under a heading, 'Limitations of producing a boardgame', she states:

> There were many minor drawbacks to this area of my project but most I managed to overcome. I am still not satisfied with the way I have presented the boardgame. I would have liked to display the game in a box but I did not allow enough time to do this.

And under the headline, 'What I have learnt from my project', Aline writes as follows:

One of the major achievements I feel I have gained through the ten months project period is the skill of keeping to deadlines and to work consistently in order to meet them. This ability has increased as my project progressed. At first, when a deadline was set, I tended to put off the work involved as the deadline was usually weeks away and ended up doing the work at the last minute. I found out that this method was not at all effective and would only cause me stress and panic that could be avoided. As time went on and more deadlines were set, I learnt to organize and spread my work over a period. I found this method of planning my work usually gained me better grades.

Also, associated with the above ability, I have learnt that the only way to achieve good grades is to organize my time; to plan out a timetable or calendar indicating days when work is due in and to organize my time around this time schedule.

Much of the research I carried out in my project involved inter-personal communication in different forms. Having interviews with people of different status; members of the public, my tutors and McDonalds' managers has taught me to communicate in various ways according to their authority and social status. To design letters in such a way to communicate effectively to the reader. I have also become aware of the different ways messages can be sent from the sender to the receiver, e.g., television, newspapers, etc.

Learning to listen to advice given to me has never been one of my assets but since July last year I have found that help and suggestions from tutors and other people advising me in my project should be taken. I hope that I have learnt to take note of other people's opinions and not to keep solely to my own without consideration for others.

By analysing material in my journal I have been able to apply class theory work to practical 'real life' situations. I feel this to be a most valuable experience as it is necessary to realize that theory work has a practical purpose.

I also feel that I have discovered skills that I previously did not realize I had.

A brief summary of the skills acquired by Aline whilst carrying out this project is as follows:

1. The development of political and social awareness
2. The designing and carrying out of questionnaires and of collating data.
3. Time management
4. Sustained prose writing
5. Self-analysis and self-assessment
6. Letter writing
7. Critical analysis of communications material
8. Interviewing
9. Telephone skills
10. Independent learning and decision-making
11. Word processing
12. Art, design and craft
13. Oral skills

Communication Studies staff at Peter Symonds' College are convinced that the materials, teaching and learning strategies and the assessment procedures, especially the project, offer a wide range of the experiences recommended in the entitlement curriculum. Skills and competences as well as critical judgement are promoted by all its demands and activities, thus preparing students for the world of work and for higher education. At a time when entitlement must also include issues of access to career opportunities through qualifications, Communication Studies has been impressively successful. The analysis of A-level grades shows Communication Studies students consistently doing as well or better than their predicted grades. Its introduction into Peter Symonds' College's portfolio of courses has, therefore, enabled many students to be in the best possible position to decide on their future careers.

Conclusion

We have, throughout this book, argued that A-level English Literature and A-level Communication Studies both offer valuable opportunities for students to experience the entitlement curriculum. Our recommended teaching and learning strategies and choice of materials aim to develop personal autonomy and a mature critical perspective on society. By these means the professed ideals of the National Curriculum can be carried upwards into the 16–19 phase. We hope it is clear that the traditional syllabus on the one hand and the innovative syllabus on the other can both provide these opportunities. Thus, constraints of syllabus alone should not dishearten the teacher eager to introduce the entitlement curriculum into her or his classroom. Our descriptions of the cooperative efforts of English departments should support teachers seeking new ways to maintain continuity with good GCSE practice, and to extend the cross-curricular component of the National Curriculum.

Entitlement and access

However, in the educational climate of the 1990s the issue of the access element of entitlement takes on a new urgency, and it is with this that we shall be primarily concerned in this concluding discussion. It will be remembered that, in our Introduction, we discussed the potential scope of entitlement in the post-16 phase, and gave examples of LEAs who had responded to the challenge of defining this concept as it applied to their institutions and the courses they offered. Unlike provision 5–16, the 16–19 phase still does not fall under any statutory order. This lack of restriction and freedom from constraint has always been both liberating and problematic. Policy-makers have always had to decide which programmes of study would be offered to students as well as how these programmes would be delivered. Whether they acknowledged it or not, they were making decisions which affected students' entitlement. In the current situation, with LEAs losing power, that responsibility is devolving upon individual institutions. The climate in which these institutions operate will become more competitive as incorporation is implemented. Management teams in colleges are already under heavy pressure from parents and governors to offer effective provision for the whole of a 16–19 constituency that is wider and more varied than ever. This they will have to do successfully in order to maintain viable student numbers.

At present, one in five students is entering higher education, a figure which, it is expected, will rise to one in three by the year 2000. The high-status academic, low-status vocational divide is as firmly in place as ever, and the likelihood is that employers will increasingly seek graduates for jobs that were formerly open to school leavers. (Professions such as accountancy, law and personnel management, which used to be open to non-graduates, are now closed to them.) Demand for A-level success, and thus entry to institutions of higher education is certain to rise. In this context, 'planning an appropriate portfolio of courses' could well become 'planning an appropriate portfolio of A-level courses' for a range of students whose parents will want them to go on to higher education in order to maximize their career opportunities. Meeting the needs of this large and varied group and the wide range of ability and educational and cultural experience they bring, poses challenging problems for institutions and their staff.

Access to A-level English: the need for choice

The trend continues to move away from the Sciences and towards the Arts and Humanities, and among these English is one of the most popular subjects. In this broad context, the career prospects for those students who choose English at A-level have to be considered. Boards offer a variety of ways of studying English at A-level: Media Studies, Theatre Studies, English Language, Communication Studies, as well as English Literature. English Literature continues to be by far the most popular for a variety of reasons: admissions policies for higher education, academic backgrounds of teaching staff, limited space, financial constraints on appropriate resources. Nonetheless, institutions do need to ask how well the interests of their students are served by English Literature syllabuses, as the majority are currently composed. As we have pointed out, the hurdle of the practical criticism paper remains a serious obstacle to successful performance for a significant number of students. Even on the most innovative syllabuses (AEB 660, Welsh, JMB) some students do not reach their full potential because of the demands of the 'Unseen'.

With this in mind it is relevant to consider the experience of Peter Symonds' College, where the planning concerns have been typical of those facing 16–19 institutions. Their decision to introduce Communication Studies was a response to the pressure of increasing student numbers and their perception of a changing student profile.

It will be remembered that we discussed the academic profile of potential candidates for the Communication Studies A-level at some length, pointing out the attraction of the subject for many students who would not normally have considered themselves 'academic'. Such students typically have lower GCSE grades than their more academic peers. Yet it has been noticeable that students on the A-level Communication Studies course achieved a higher grade than that predicted for them, and a higher grade than in their other A-level subjects.

These results in A-level Communication Studies are not due to any incommensurability between the content or the assessment criteria of different subjects: the material of A-level Communication Studies is conceptually as taxing as that of any other A-level subject. Rather, they are the consequence of the students' own enthusiasm for the subject, both in its content and in the freedom they are given to follow their own areas of interest. It is this combination of choice and interesting subject matter that fosters their strong sense of commitment to the course.

Post-18 entitlement

Such good results in A-level Communication Studies are encouraging, suggesting as they do that the pragmatic goals that all institutions need to consider (examination results) can still be combined with idealistic ones (enhancing the student's educational experience).

For responsible schools and colleges, part of students' entitlement will mean ensuring that they are able to make appropriate decisions from the widest possible range of choices after leaving their educational institution. This will include the vocational as well as the academic route. Enough has been said in this book about the opportunities offered by A-level English Literature and A-level Communication Studies subjects to equip students with the skills and competences that imaginative teaching can develop. What can we say, however, about the courses available to students post-18 for which these two subjects are appropriate preparations? Little need be said about English Literature courses, though increasingly these can be taken in conjunction with Media and Cultural Studies, some of whose theory and content draws on the areas discussed in A-level Communication Studies. It is also noticeable that, in the last 10 years, Communication Studies is offered by an increasing number of universities and can now be studied in a range of combinations. Sometimes the subject takes a practical form, sometimes it appears as an academic and theoretical discipline. In Universities' guides, Communication Studies now appears in combination with Languages, Business Management and Public Relations. By 1991, Admissions Officers were reporting that there was a higher demand for Media and Communication Studies degrees than for any other courses. It can be fairly claimed, then, that both A-level English Literature and A-level Communication Studies give students an adequate preparation for a variety of courses in higher education.

With vocational routes in mind, the experience of introducing A-level Communication Studies at Peter Symonds' College is again worth noting. Often, the work done on the Communication Studies course, and particularly on the project, stimulates and advances the personal interest of a student to such a degree that he or she goes on to choose a career on that basis. A number of students whose projects involved working with children in schools have gone on to train as teachers. In one case, a student actually discovered her vocation through her project: choosing to study and work with handicapped children in a local Special School convinced her that she wanted to continue work with disabled children, and after completing her A-level course she enrolled on a nursing programme with special provision for the disabled. Another student whose project involved investigating the treatment of young offenders was offered a university place to study for a law degree.

We have had a 'new' sixth for the last two decades, and curriculum history since then is littered with failed attempts to respond to its needs; there have been Q and F, N and F, CEE, the Higginson recommendations, the introduction of 'AS' level and proposals to introduce core skills. All of these have failed to achieve the goals set by reformers. Official support for the 'gold standard' of the A-level examination is as strong as ever, and the gulf between academic and vocational provision remains wide. The concept of entitlement emerged as part of a generous attempt once again to provide an education of high quality for the increasingly large 16–19 cohort.

As we have defined it in this book, there seem to be two possible ways of combining English with entitlement while A-levels persist in their present form. Teachers can work within existing syllabuses, in ways that we have suggested, to embed entitlement values. Institutions can, as Peter Symonds' College has done, provide courses that offer the best chance of examination success for the great majority of their students.

Appendix 1

One of the first schemes directly to assess the possibility of delivering entitlement through the A-level curriculum was initiated in 1988, by a group of Northern LEAs: Bradford, Humberside, Newcastle, North Tyneside and Sunderland. Here, an ambitious programme to consider introducing elements of the entitlement curriculum into 14 A-levels was set up. The project was linked with BTEC, FEU, JMB, London University Institute of Education and the Training Agency. Their aims were expressed in the following terms:

> The purpose of the proposed project is to develop 'A' level schemes which contribute to the core entitlement and provide the flexibility that allows the negotiation of the curriculum and recording of achievement demanded by student-centred learning. . . . [The core entitlements are] Numeracy, Communications, Science and Technology, Information Technology, Enterprise and Economic Awareness, Social, Political and Cultural Awareness, Creative Skills, Student-Centred Learning, Recording of Achievement, Problem Solving, Equality of Opportunity, Learning Skills, Personal Development/Effectiveness, Guidance and Counselling (including Careers Guidance), Open Learning/Supported Self-Study, Values and Attitudes, Leisure and Recreational Activities, Experience of Work, Industry Links, Aesthetic Awareness (Yorkshire LEA, 1988).

Developments to introduce the entitlement curriculum into the 16–19 cohort in Leicestershire were to some extent inspired by the work of the Northern LEAs. The statement on the development of post-16 entitlement in Leicestershire began by quoting the LEA's Curriculum Statement and went on to tease out its implications for the whole of the 16–19 curriculum.

Leicestershire LEA's Curriculum Statement (1989)

> . . . all learners in Leicestershire schools, colleges and centres are entitled to a planned curriculum which is broad, balanced, relevant, differentiated, coherent, which has continuity and which is participative.

This statement applied to pupils and students of all ages. When developed for the post-16 cohort, the A-level Enhancement Project set out the following elements which were seen as defining the entitlement of each student:

1. A personal, negotiated programme, balanced in process, context and content, which builds on the experience and interests of the learner.
2. Guidance and counselling, to include a structure for personal tutoring.
3. A planned programme of personal and social education, to include continued development of cross-curricular themes and dimensions identified in National Curriculum Council Circular 6 (economic & industrial understanding, careers education and guidance, environmental education, health education, citizenship).
4. The continued development of core skills – Communication skills; Communication and information handling skills (including graphics, numeracy, information technology, media, foreign language); Organisation and management skills (including personal management and effectiveness, study skills); Practical and creative skills; Decision making and problem solving skills.

It went on:

The negotiated, balanced learning programme for each student will make use of a range of teaching and learning styles, including:

supported self-study
distance learning
individual research and enquiry–project work
the use of information technology
directed and self-directed assignments
group work
formal instruction.

The LEA's policy statement went on to state that:

access to the styles and elements described above should make use of a variety of learning environments. In addition to the school or college these will include:

work place
other schools/colleges
further and higher education
the community
residential experience
field studies.

In terms of a recommended implementation strategy, the LEA came out firmly in favour of curriculum embedding:

The concept of 'entitlement' to a curriculum which embraces these opportunities implies that they will not take the form of 'bolt on' extras, but will be available through a combination of mainstream studies (i.e. A levels, BTEC, GCSEs, CPVE, etc.) and such additional studies as may be necessary to guarantee access to entitlement.

Finally, the entitlement programme was to be linked to other processes which it was hoped would be extended into the 16–19 range:

Central to the concept of an entitlement curriculum is the Record of Achievement, which is both a summative record of what a student has achieved and a formative document upon which is based individual review and the negotiation of a personal action plan.

Implementation of this statement came with the setting up of teams of specialist teachers recruited from schools and colleges, each working on an A-level subject. Teachers on this initiative experimented in the main with existing syllabuses, seeking ways to embed the entitlement programme within these traditional frameworks. Material was produced that gave guidance on student-centred, flexible teaching and learning styles, and the issue of students' awareness of themes and issues in the wider world was addressed by introducing appropriate material into prescribed courses of study. These themes and issues show a slightly more ambitious scope than those of the Northern group: Economic/industrial understanding, careers education, environmental education, health education, citizenship, equal opportunities, political/social awareness, visual/aesthetic awareness, scientific/technological understanding.

Finally, so that the reader can see the element of consonance that runs through all entitlement statements, here are the themes included in the Cambridgeshire LEA statement (1989):

> Economic, Industrial and Community Awareness, Environmental Awareness, Society (organisation and structure), Health Education, Moral Awareness, Awareness of Scientific and Technological Applications, Creative and Aesthetic Understanding, Equal Opportunities.

References

Cambridgeshire LEA (1989) Entitlement document, author.
Leicestershire LEA (1989) *Post-16 Entitlement in Leicestershire – Some Practical Implications*, County Hall, Glenfield, Leicester.
Yorkshire LEA (1988) *Proposed Joint Project between Yorkshire and Humberside and North East Region. TVEI Projects*, Bradford: Yorkshire LEA.

Appendix 2

Communication studies – 608*

(*Available in June only)
SYLLABUS – ADVANCED LEVEL

Two papers, each of 3 hours, a project and an oral test

1. Aims of the Syllabus

A course based on this syllabus should promote knowledge of, understanding of, and competence in communication by:

1.1 study of categories, forms and uses of communication, in order to interpret major theories and issues;

1.2 application of this study to cases drawn from authentic situations;

1.3 development of practical skills in communication.

2. Assessment Objectives

The examination will assess a candidate's ability to demonstrate knowledge, understanding, and skills in the three areas of activity described under the 'aims of the syllabus' by:

2.1 showing knowledge and understanding of major theories of intrapersonal, interpersonal, group, mass and extrapersonal communication; (1.1)

2.2 showing knowledge and understanding of major contemporary political, economic and social issues in communication; (1.1)

2.3 showing knowledge and understanding of the interaction between people and machines and of current or potential development in communication technology; (1.1)

2.4 offering description and interpretation of communication in a given context; (1.2)

2.5 playing a communication role or roles in a given context or contexts; (1.2)

2.6 applying relevant theories to cases; (1.2)

2.7 applying understanding of issues to cases; (1.2)

2.8 demonstrating, through case studies (paper 2) and the project (paper 3), the ability to use communication skills and techniques accurately and appropriately in a wide range of means of communication; (1.2/1.3)

2.9 using these skills and techniques to show awareness of factors which influence the communication process. (1.3)

3. Assessment Pattern

Two three-hour papers, externally examined, plus a project, which will be internally examined, and Board moderated. Paper 1 will receive 40% of the total marks. Papers 2 and 3 will each receive 30% of the total marks.

3.1 Paper 1

There will be two sections, A and B. Four questions are to be answered, one of which will be from Section A, and three from Section B. A choice of questions will be offered in both Sections.

A variety of forms of communication may be offered for some questions.

Graphic and diagrammatic responses may be required, as well as the standard essay, or a number of short questions.

3.2 Paper 2 – Case Study

One or two Case Studies may be offered. If only one Case Study is offered, candidates will be given a choice of roles and tasks.

Candidates collect stimulus material two days before the examination. They may make notes on this material for use in the examination. They may not, however, take extra pieces of material into the examination room.

Questions will test the ability to adapt theories and/or models to practical situations, to adopt a mode or modes of communication appropriate to a particular role or roles, and to evaluate the case study materials.

3.3 Paper 3 – Project

20% of the total examination marks will be awarded for the work, the diary/log, and for written assessment by the candidate.

10% of the total examination marks will be awarded for a short individual oral presentation relating to the project work and its creation, and for effective participation in a subsequent group discussion.

The project must be original in execution, if not in source material.

It must be in an acceptable form which demonstrates competence in achieving the objectives stated above.

External Candidates

It is regretted that, in view of the special administrative and assessment requirements for Paper 2 and the project, the examination will not be available to external candidates.

Further information concerning this syllabus is available on request from The Secretary General.

4. Subject Content

The subject content describes subjects of enquiry and practice. These areas should be seen as contributing collectively to the study of the communications process in a range of possible situations.

Guidance Notes

4.1 Categories of Communication

4.1.1 Intrapersonal Communication: the study of the communication process within the individual, and as it relates to other categories.
Includes concepts such as self-image, self-esteem, and the processes of perception, cognition, and the generation of meanings.

4.1.2 Interpersonal Communication: including the study of dyadic communication, and factors affecting this process in a wide range of situations.
Includes such factors as perception, culture, experience, performance, self-presentation.

4.1.3 Extrapersonal Communication; including communication through and to non-human and inanimate sources and resources.
Includes the nature of communication between people and machines, including the development of machine intelligence.

4.1.4 Group Communication: including distinctions between large and small groups; formal and informal groups; ways in which communication is used by groups within themselves and others; communication within and between institutions.
Includes ways in which formal and informal groups use communication to achieve goals, reinforce norms, and display identity. Study of institutions includes the handling of information and decision-making, and the problems of maintaining effective communication within and between large groups.

4.1.5 Mass Communication: including study of the mass media and the institutions, characteristics, and effects of kinds of mass communication.
Includes such mass media as radio, television and the press and such concepts as access, control, audience, mediation and stereotyping.

4.2 Forms of Communication

4.2.1 Oral communication.
Includes individual presentation; types of two-way exchange (for example, interviews); types of discussion (for example, debates); recognition of paralinguistic features (for example, tone and intonation, accent, stress).

4.2.2 Written and printed communication.
Includes texts in a wide variety of styles and registers.

4.2.3 Non-verbal communication.
Includes the effects and uses of body language, dress and display cues.

Recognition of its importance for communicating roles, attitudes and emotions.

4.2.4 Graphical communication.
Includes graphics in their pictorial and symbolic modes; analysis of ways (including conventions) by which images are constructed, as well as sequences of images (visual narrative).

4.2.5 Numerical communication.
Includes the application and significance of systems of number, and the presentation and interpretation of data in numerical form.

4.2.6 New technologies.
Includes appreciation of the uses and effects of communication technologies; information technology; the personal and social implications of new technologies. Opportunities are provided for detailed technical knowledge to be used as, for example, in computer studies.

4.3 Uses of Communication

4.3.1 Information gathering, storage, retrieval, dissemination.
Includes definitions of the term 'information'; kinds of public access to information sources; ways of expressing information through various media; the processing of information by institutions; kinds of power conferred by possession, control and marketing of information.

4.3.2 Socialisation.
Includes the production of values through communication; the reinforcement of norms in groups and institutions; the acquisition of individual roles; the integration of the individual into social groups; the part that communication plays in constructing social reality; political awareness and activity.

4.3.3 Social functioning.
Includes study of expressive and affiliative needs, and personal growth, relating particularly to the categories of interpersonal and group communications; creative expression in the arts.

4.4 Theory in Communication Studies

4.4.1 Identification of basic factors; description of principles; discussion of hypotheses; uses and limitations of models.
Area of study includes theories presented within the four divisions described, for example the concept of need operating as a factor across a range of communication situations (Berlo); the principle that context of reception always affects understanding of communication (Schramm); the hypothesis that communication may be understood as an instrument of control (Smith); the 'advocacy' model as a means of understanding how politics are mediated through television (Tracey).
It should be made clear that in respect of models in particular, criticism of existing models is to be encouraged, as is the production of original models.

4.4.2 Description and interpretation of the communication process in a variety of situations.

4.4.3 Description and interpretation of the development of mass communications from the late nineteenth century and of the significance of this for contemporary society, and for the future.

4.5 Issues in Communication Studies

Description and discussion of those issues raised by communications activity within political, economic, social, and cultural spheres.

Issues in communication studies are public debates of an ethical, moral, political, or social nature that are defined by agencies such as the media, the education system, and organs of public discussion. (Examples include the question of control of and access to electronic means of information storage and questions relating to the production of gender stereotypes through the media.) Particular reference will be made to those issues concerned with the organisation, functioning, and effects of mass communication, as well as to those issues relating to the impact of technology on communication experienced by the individual and by society as a whole.